W9-BRU-097

FERGUSON
CAREER BIOGRAPHIES

MICHAEL
JORDAN

Basketball Player

Mike McGovern

Ferguson
An imprint of ☑️ Facts On File

Michael Jordan: Basketball Player

Copyright © 2005 by Facts On File, Inc.

Ferguson
An imprint of Facts On File, Inc.
132 West 31st Street
New York NY 10001

Library of Congress Cataloging-in-Publication Data

McGovern, Mike, 1954–
  Michael Jordan : basketball player / Mike McGovern.
    p. cm.
  Includes bibliographical references and index.
  ISBN 0-8160-5876-8 (hc : alk. paper)
 1. Jordan, Michael, 1963– 2. Basketball players—United States—Biography. I. Title.
  GV884.J63M34 2005
  796.323′092—dc22   2004003955

Text design by David Strelecky

Pages 104–129 adapted from Ferguson's *Encyclopedia of Careers and Vocational Guidance, Twelfth Edition*

Printed in the United States of America

MP Hermitage 10 9 8 7 6 5 4 3 2 1

This book is printed on acid-free paper.

CONTENTS

1

THE FACE OF PROFESSIONAL BASKETBALL

Even if you are not an avid basketball fan, or much of a sports fan at all, chances are you know something about Michael Jordan. You might know him as the player with the gleaming bald head who defies gravity and makes the impossible look routine on the court. You might know him as a spokesperson for Nike, Hanes underwear, Ball Park Franks, Gatorade, and McDonald's. Or you might know him as a movie star: His 1996 film, *Space Jam,* co-starring Bugs Bunny and Daffy Duck, was a box office smash.

Michael Jordan is one of those rare athletes who tran-scends his sport, because he was so very good at it. Many people believe he was the best player ever to play the game. And Jordan always played with flair, passion, and a will to win that was unsurpassed by any athlete in any sport.

He set an example for his teammates—and was a role model to kids—with his tireless work ethic, his diligence at practice, and his refusal to let his success go to his head. Jordan never went half speed and never played the game with anything but a singular focus. So when the best player in the game was always trying to improve, it figured that the rest of his teammates would do what was necessary to keep up.

It is no surprise then that Jordan, in spite of his many individual accomplishments, was regarded as a true team player: someone who made his teammates better. It is also no surprise that Jordan led the Chicago Bulls to six National Basketball Association (NBA) championships in an eight-year span.

For many people, Jordan was the face of professional basketball. If his team was on television, people would tune in, because there was always the chance—a good chance—that they'd see something unforgettable: a thunderous slam dunk, an improvised drive to the basket, or a last-second, beat-the-buzzer game-winning shot. He was a one-man highlight film.

But Jordan would not have been nearly so popular on the court had he not been such a model citizen off the court. He understood the responsibility he had as the most visible player in his sport, and he conducted himself accordingly: with class and dignity.

Throughout his famous career, Michael Jordan became the face of professional basketball for millions of fans. (Photofest)

But for all his accomplishments, and for as easy as he made things look as a pro, Jordan initially struggled with the game, believe it or not. But even as a child, he was driven by his determination to excel. He would accept nothing less than success— a characteristic that would be the keystone of his career.

2

HUMBLE BEGINNINGS

Michael Jordan's strong work ethic is in his genes. His father, James, and his mother, Deloris, both the children of Southern farmers, worked hard to ensure that their five children had what they needed.

Michael was born on February 17, 1963, in Brooklyn, New York, where his father was enrolled in a training program at General Electric. The family returned to North Carolina after the training program was complete and settled in Wilmington.

In addition to his job with General Electric and building the family a new house, James still found time to be involved with his children. He encouraged their participation in all sports. In fact, Michael's first love was Little League baseball. But soon basketball became his favorite sport.

James built a makeshift basketball court in the backyard. It was nothing fancy, just backboards and baskets. It was not long before "the Rack," as the court came to be known, was the second home for Michael and his older brother, Larry.

They played against each other for hours at a time, and Larry took no pity on his little brother. But who won or lost was not as important as the fun they had together. Their fun depended on Larry and Michael keeping up

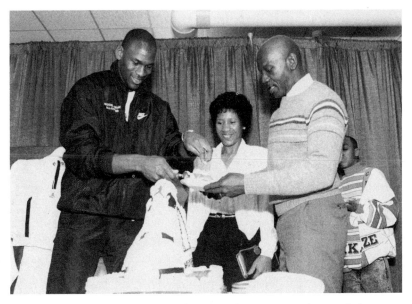

Michael and his parents, Deloris and James Jordan, celebrate Michael's 26th birthday. (Associated Press)

with their schoolwork, though; Michael and his siblings learned at an early age the importance of education.

The All-Around Athlete

By the time Michael was a sophomore at Laney High School, he had grown to 5'10", much taller than anyone else in his family. He had become an all-round athlete, playing football and running track. He also expected to be a member of the varsity basketball team, but Coach Clifton Herring cut Jordan from the team. The best he could do was the junior varsity.

Michael was so disappointed that he actually considered giving up basketball. But that decision would have gone against all his parents' preaching about the value of hard work and determination. So instead of quitting, he worked even harder. At the end of the season, Michael led the junior varsity team by averaging 28 points a game.

"Whenever I was working out and got tired and figured I ought to stop," Jordan told Larry Schwartz of ESPN.com, "I'd close my eyes and see that list in the locker room without my name on it, and that usually got me going again."

That is exactly what happened. During his junior and senior seasons at Laney, Jordan developed into one of the best players in North Carolina. He played so well that he earned an invitation to the prestigious Five Star Basketball Camp in Pittsburgh, Pennsylvania in the summer following his junior year. The Five Star Camp played host to many of the finest high school basketball players in the United States and was attended by college basketball coaches interested in evaluating potential recruits.

Jordan, who was surprised to receive an invitation, arrived at the camp without any of the college coaches knowing who he was. But before long he got their attention and began making a name for himself. He won five trophies during the first week of camp and four more during the second. By the time the camp was over, he was one of the best players there.

Jordan began receiving calls and letters from college coaches, wanting him to play for their school. After seriously considering a scholarship offer from North Carolina State, where his favorite player, David Thompson, had gone to school, Jordan announced he would attend the University of North Carolina at Chapel Hill, where he would play for the Tar Heels under legendary coach Dean Smith.

Smith, who went on to become the winningest basketball coach in the history of the National Collegiate Athletic Association (NCAA), emphasized fundamentals, team play, discipline, and the importance of education. Jordan credits Smith with his development as a basketball player and as a person.

The Legend Begins

Just a year earlier at the Five Star Camp, Michael Jordan was virtually unknown as a basketball player. But his improvement since that time had been dramatic.

After averaging just under 28 points a game for Laney High School during his senior season, Jordan came to Chapel Hill and made an immediate impact. He became just the fourth freshman at North Carolina to start his first game. (In basketball, *to start* means to be part of the first group of players on the court.) And although Jordan later became famous for his offensive skills—his ability to soar through the air, his acrobatic dunks, his slashes to the basket—he became one of the few freshmen ever to start in his first game at North Carolina because of his defense.

Jordan averaged 13.5 points a game as a freshman and was named to the *Basketball Weekly* All-Freshman Team. The Tar Heels won the Atlantic Coast Conference (ACC) championship that season and made it to the 1982 NCAA Basketball Championship Tournament. They advanced to the title game against the Georgetown Hoyas in the Louisiana Superdome in New Orleans.

The game was one of the most memorable championship games ever played. It was very close from start to finish. Neither team was able to build a comfortable margin.

With 32 seconds to play and Georgetown leading 62-61, Coach Smith called a timeout. He instructed the players to look for the first good shot and to get in good rebounding position. Just before the timeout ended, Smith tapped Jordan on the knee and said, "Knock it in, Michael."

Before 61,612 roaring fans, Michael—a freshman—had been asked to take the most important shot of the season. The inbounds pass went to point guard Jimmy Black, who passed to forward Matt Doherty, who passed the ball back to Black. Black spotted Jordan on his left, about 17 feet from the basket, midway between the foul line and the sideline.

Jordan did not hesitate. He gathered the pass, took aim, released the ball perfectly, and never saw the result.

"I actually closed my eyes," he said. "Something I'd never done before. I honestly did not know that the shot had gone in until Georgetown took the ball out of bounds."

Several seconds later, after a Georgetown turnover, the Tar Heels were 63-62 winners. Michael Jordan's pressure-packed shot had given Dean Smith his first national championship.

"The kid doesn't even realize it yet, but he's part of history now," Eddie Fogler, an assistant coach at North Carolina, said after the game. "People will remember that shot 25 years from now."

Jordan recalled the 1982 national championship game in his book, *For the Love of the Game.* "I knew the magnitude of the game, but I didn't fully comprehend what it meant. . . . I remember riding to the arena. There I was about to fall asleep on the bus and I'm daydreaming about hitting a winning shot.

"I remember feeling so calm, so relaxed. I wasn't completely awake and I wasn't completely asleep. I was in a comfortable place somewhere in between. I envisioned being the hero in a game. I saw myself hitting the game-winning shot. . . . The dream wasn't specific; I didn't know whether it would be against Georgetown in a few hours or against another team in another year.

"But after we beat Georgetown for the championship, I told my father about the dream. He paused for a moment and said: 'Your life will never be the same after that shot. Your life is going to change, son.'

"I thought, 'Well that's just my father talking. Of course, he's going to think that about his son.' And besides, no one really knows one way or another."

As it turned out, James Jordan was exactly right.

What Sophomore Jinx?

An athlete who starts as a freshman often fails to repeat his or her performance as a sophomore. This is often referred to as the *sophomore jinx.*

Not surprisingly, Michael Jordan did just fine during the 1982–83 season as a sophomore. He increased his

Michael first made a name for himself playing for the University of North Carolina Tar Heels. (Landov)

scoring average from 13.5 to 20 points a game. He also averaged more than five rebounds and two steals a game.

One of his most important steals came in a game against an ACC rival, the Virginia Cavaliers. Trailing by 10 points with four minutes to play, North Carolina scored the last 11 points of the game. Jordan made a basket that brought the Tar Heels within one point, and then with about a minute left, he made a steal and a dunk to win the game.

North Carolina failed to repeat as national champions in 1983, finishing the season with a 28-8 record (28 wins and eight losses) and falling one game short of qualifying for the NCAA Final Four (the last weekend of the NCAA basketball tournament, when the four final teams face off).

Following the Tar Heels' season-ending loss to the University of Georgia Bulldogs in the 1983 NCAA East Regional final, Jordan was so disappointed that he ended up in the gym the night the team returned home. As far as he was concerned, there was no time to waste in trying to improve.

Jordan was named to several All-America teams and was chosen National Player of the Year by _The Sporting News,_ a weekly magazine. That summer, he was the leading scorer on the U.S. Pan American Games team, which won the gold medal in Caracas, Venezuela.

Farewell to Chapel Hill

Michael's junior year at North Carolina turned out to be his last. The Tar Heels, who entered the season ranked first in most polls, won their first 21 games and finished 28-3. They qualified for the NCAA Tournament once again, but just like in 1983, their season ended in disappointment.

After North Carolina beat the Temple University Owls in its first-round NCAA game, the next opponent was the Indiana Hoosiers, coached by Bob Knight, one of the most respected coaches in the country. Using a style of play that was deliberate and disciplined, the Hoosiers contained Jordan, limiting him to 13 points and one rebound, in a 72-68 upset.

Still, the season was full of awards and praise for Jordan. He averaged 19.6 points a game to lead the ACC in scoring. He was named the ACC Player of the Year; he was a unanimous choice for National Player of the Year; and he was a choice for every All-America team that year.

For his career at North Carolina, Jordan averaged 17.7 points and five rebounds a game. He was on two ACC championship teams and one NCAA championship team. He also won just about every individual award handed out. So it came time to make a decision about his future: stay at North Carolina for his senior year or turn pro and make himself eligible for the big time: the National Basketball Association (NBA).

From the start, Coach Smith was in favor of Jordan bypassing his final year of college eligibility and moving on to the NBA. Smith knew Jordan's game was tailor-made for the NBA. Michael's parents were less enthusiastic, because they understood the importance of education and wanted him to get his degree.

After much agonizing, Michael decided to leave North Carolina. The announcement did not sit well with many fans and alumni, who wanted Jordan to remain a Tar Heel and lead a team that figured to be one of the nation's best. But Smith defended Jordan's decision, saying what was most important was what was best for Jordan.

"That was when I felt Coach Smith was more like a father than anything else," Jordan said. "I wasn't going to the NBA until he advised me to do it."

Jordan promised his parents that even though he was leaving college, he would return to earn his degree. In 1985, he did just that, graduating from North Carolina with a bachelor's degree in geography.

Despite declaring his intentions to turn pro, Jordan had one more obligation as an amateur: He was chosen to represent the United States as a member of the 1984 U.S. men's Olympic basketball team, which, in those days, consisted entirely of college players.

Jordan was the team's leading scorer, averaging 17 points a game, and the United States routed Spain to win the gold medal.

Now it was time for Michael to start thinking about basketball as a job, not an extracurricular activity. His future home and career depended on one thing: the NBA draft.

3

NEXT STOP:
CHICAGO

Each summer, the NBA conducts a draft, allowing its teams to select from college players and international players. Teams select in inverse order of their finish in the standings. In other words, the poorer a team's record, the earlier in the draft it gets to select. At least that was the procedure in 1984, prior to the institution of the draft lottery, which is in effect today.

As the season drew to a close, it looked as if Michael Jordan would be selected by either the Houston Rockets, the Portland Trail Blazers, the Chicago Bulls, or the Philadelphia 76ers.

When the standings were final, the worst team in the Eastern Conference, Houston, and the worst team from the Western Conference, Portland, had a coin flip to determine who would make the first choice. Houston won the flip and selected Hakeem Olajuwon of the Uni-

versity of Houston. Port-
land, picking second,
went for Sam Bowie of the
University of Kentucky.
Chicago, the team with
the third worst record,
regardless of conference,
selected Jordan.

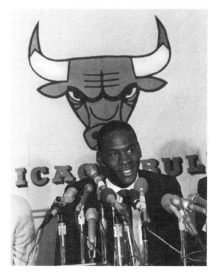

Looking back, it is difficult to fathom now that
Michael Jordan, arguably
the greatest player ever to
play basketball, was not
even the number one draft
choice when he left col-

*Speaking to the press after
being drafted by the Chicago
Bulls in 1984* (Associated Press)

lege. It was not long before he proved that Houston and
Portland made serious errors in judgment.

Jordan the Rookie

When Michael Jordan entered his first training camp in
September 1984 with the Chicago Bulls, he did so with
only one goal in mind: to impress.

"I wanted to impress my teammates, my coaches, the
owners, everybody," Jordan wrote in *For the Love of the
Game*. "I wanted them to say: 'This kid is special. This kid
has the right mind, the right skills, the right motivation.'

All my effort that first year was geared toward proving myself. I went as hard as I could all the time. I tried to win every drill, every scrimmage."

The work ethic and determination Jordan displayed in high school and college were not forgotten once he reached the NBA. He actually seemed to be more intense and more driven. He was not vocal as a rookie; he knew his place and understood the hierarchy of an NBA team. So instead of leading by his words, he led by his actions.

During his rookie season, Jordan was spectacular. He not only made a name for himself, but he brought considerable attention to the league. Fans tuned in, because they never knew what Jordan would do that had not been done before—by anyone. With his ability to take off at the foul line and seemingly soar through the air, Jordan was his own nightly highlight film.

Adding to Jordan's appeal was the endorsement contract he signed with the sneaker company Nike, which created and publicized a shoe just for him—Air Jordans. The brand grossed $130 million in its first year on the market. The shoe was red and black, but because it did not conform to the rest of the Bulls uniform guidelines, the NBA prohibited Michael from wearing the shoe. Jordan ignored the ban, and the fines piled up, starting at $1,000 a game, then escalating to $3,000, and finally $5,000 a game. Jordan kept wearing the shoes and Nike willingly paid the fines, because it was less expensive than paying to promote the shoes on television or the print media.

Jordan's shoes became wildly popular, as did his number 23 Bulls jersey. Kids throughout country, wanting to "be like Mike," even started sticking their tongues out while they played, copying a habit Jordan developed as a kid.

In addition to making an impact at the ticket office and on playgrounds from coast to coast, Jordan was making his presence felt in every game he played.

A Star Is Born

In just the first half of the 1984–85 season, Michael Jordan led the Bulls to 23 wins. They had just 27 wins total in the previous season. His performance was good enough to earn him a starting spot in the NBA All-Star Game in Indianapolis, Indiana. But what should have been a time for celebration turned into one of the most hurtful episodes of his career.

Several of the more established players in the league— Isiah Thomas of the Detroit Pistons and Dominique Wilkins of the Atlanta Hawks, in particular—were not happy that Jordan chose the Slam Dunk competition, a contest in which players compete to see who can perform the best slam dunk, to debut his Air Jordan sweats. Jordan

During his 1984–85 rookie season, Michael's strong drive to succeed brought him national attention. (Associated Press)

and Nike thought it would be the perfect time, considering all the attention the contest generated. Thomas and Wilkins thought he was being disrespectful.

Also that weekend, Jordan got onto an elevator that contained a group of NBA stars. Because Michael was unsure of what to say to them, given some of the static he had already received, he chose to play it safe and not say a thing. His silence was perceived as a snub.

When it came time for the game, the players decided to freeze out Jordan. They did not pass him the ball when he was open; nor did they help him when the defense surrounded him. In Jordan's 22 minutes of play, he attempted just nine shots.

Jordan thought long and hard about the freeze-out and spent a long time talking to his parents about it.

"I knew that everything happened for a purpose and I could either learn from the experience or fight it," Jordan said. "I decided to do both."

The Bulls' next regular season game was against the Pistons in Detroit, and Jordan let Thomas know exactly how he felt about the All-Star snub. He led the Bulls to an overtime victory, scoring 49 points, grabbing 15 rebounds, and partially blocking Thomas's last-second shot that would have tied the game.

For the next seven years, the rivalry between the Bulls and the Pistons was as fierce as any in the NBA.

A Return to the Playoffs

Over the last 30 games of the regular season, Chicago, with a record of 38-44, played well enough to qualify for the NBA playoffs for the first time since 1981. Michael Jordan was the Bulls' leading scorer in 24 of those games.

For the season, he led the Bulls in scoring, rebounding, assists, and steals, and he was named the NBA Rookie of the Year.

The Bulls were eliminated in the first round by the Milwaukee Bucks, who won the best-of-five series in four games. But instead of being a novelty, making the playoffs would become routine for Chicago—thanks to Jordan, who concluded a remarkable rookie season that was a sign of great things to come.

A Bad Break

Over the summer of 1985, the Chicago Bulls were sold to Jerry Reinsdorf, who also owned a Major League Baseball team, the Chicago White Sox. With the sale came a new coach, Stan Albeck, and several other personnel changes. The Bulls began the season with a new look and wins in their first two games. They also won their third game of the year, but lost their superstar in the process.

On October 29, 1985, in a game against the Golden State Warriors, Michael Jordan broke a bone in his left foot. X rays did not show the break, but Jordan felt the pain. He was hardly able to walk. It was not until he underwent a CAT scan that the break was discovered. Jordan was so depressed over the injury that his father flew to Chicago from North Carolina to cheer him up.

Initially, Jordan expected to be back in time for the NBA All-Star Game, which is played in mid-February, but after seven weeks the break still had not sufficiently healed. Michael decided to take matters into his own hands. He convinced his doctor to place a removable splint on his foot instead of a cast. Even though doctors told him not to play, he went home to North Carolina and played anyway.

Over the next four weeks, Jordan got himself back into shape; he was in such good shape that by the time he made his next visit to the doctor, his left foot was stronger than his right. He was finally cleared to play on March 15, 1986, after missing 64 games.

Fortunately for Jordan, that was the first—and last—serious injury he suffered during his years with the Chicago Bulls. In fact, from his return in March 1986 until he left the Bulls in 1998, Jordan missed only seven other games.

High Praise from a Legend

Despite playing without Michael Jordan for all but 18 games of the 1985–86 season, the Bulls managed to qualify for the NBA playoffs with a 30-52 record. Their first-round opponent was the Boston Celtics, who lost to the Los Angeles Lakers in the 1985 NBA Finals and would go on to become the NBA champs in 1986.

The Celtics won the best-of-five series in three games, but Jordan was spectacular in defeat. In Game 1 of the series, he scored 49 points in a 123-104 loss. But that was nothing compared to Game 2, won by Boston 135-131 in double overtime. Jordan played 53 minutes and made 22-of-41 field goal attempts and 19-of-21 foul shots for 63 points.

After the game, the Celtics' Larry Bird, one of the greatest players in NBA history, said this about Jordan: "I think he's God disguised as Michael Jordan. He is the most awesome player in the NBA. Today in Boston Garden, on national TV, in the playoffs, he put on one of the greatest shows of all time. I couldn't believe someone could do that against the Boston Celtics."

At the start of the 1986–87 season, Michael Jordan proved that he could do great things against anybody.

Making His Points

Michael Jordan entered his third NBA season knowing that if the Bulls were going to be successful, he would have to lead the team in scoring. He said the 1986–87 team had less physical talent than either of the two previous squads.

Going for one of many great shots (Photofest)

That left it up to him to carry the scoring load, and he rose to his own challenge.

In the season-opener against the New York Knicks, Jordan set the tone by scoring 50 points. Over the next 19 games, he failed to top 40 points only six times. His run of nine consecutive games of 40 or more points, from November 28 through December 12, 1986, was the third-longest such streak in NBA history. Wilt Chamberlain, the 7'1" center who spent most of his Hall of Fame career with the Philadelphia 76ers and Los Angeles Lakers, held the first- and second-place spots with streaks of 14 and 10 games.

Everyone knew Jordan was the Bulls offense, and everyone knew that he would be taking most of the shots. But there was no stopping him. He was the team's leading scorer in all but four of the 82 regular season games, including a then-club-record 61 points against Detroit. He scored 50 or more points five times, 40 or more 29 times, and 30 or more 28 times.

For the season, Jordan led the NBA in scoring, averaging 37.1 points a game. He set club records for points (3,041), field goals (1,098), field goal attempts (2,279), free throws (833), and free throw attempts (972). And to show that he played hard on defense as well, he set the record for steals (236).

The Bulls finished 40-42 and qualified for the playoffs for the third straight season. Once again, their first-round opponent was the Boston Celtics, the defending NBA champion. And once again, the Celtics eliminated Chicago in three games.

Despite his individual brilliance on the court, Jordan was being criticized because the Bulls were not a better team, especially in the playoffs, where great players are defined. After three straight first-round playoff sweeps, Chicago seemed nowhere close to winning an NBA championship. But that would begin to change in the 1987 draft, when the team laid the foundation for what would become a dynasty.

4

PLAYOFF SUCCESS

In the 1987 draft, the Bulls selected Horace Grant from Clemson University, and they traded for the draft rights of Scottie Pippen from Central Arkansas. Grant provided size (6'10", 245 pounds), strength, toughness, rebounding, and a defensive presence; Pippen possessed all-around skills, quickness, and great athleticism. Their addition filled two voids in the Bulls lineup and gave Michael some much-needed help.

A Commitment to Defense

The Bulls won 12 of their first 15 games in the 1987–88 season. Jordan still did most of the scoring, but with Pippen and Grant in the lineup, at least the opposition had to consider other offensive threats.

The team finished the regular season with their best record (50-32) since the 1973–74 season. Jordan led the league in scoring for the second straight year, averaging 35 points a game. He was named Most Valuable Player (MVP), All-NBA first-team, and MVP of the All-Star Game. But the 1987–88 season saw Jordan make a commitment to defense. Known mostly for his offensive prowess, Jordan understood that defense would be a way to set him apart from greats such as Larry Bird and Magic Johnson.

"They were great all-around players, but they were never known as great defenders," Jordan said. "I realized defense could be my way of separating myself from them. I decided I wanted to be recognized as a player who could influence the game at either end of the floor. . . . After the 1987–88 season the critics had to say: 'This kid can have an influence at both ends of the court. He's not just a scorer.' "

Jordan's commitment to defense was rewarded by winning the NBA's Defensive Player of the Year award. In addition to leading the league in points, he also led the league in steals, averaging 3.2 a game.

For the first time since Jordan joined the Bulls, the team entered the playoffs, not as underdogs, but as favorites. Chicago defeated the Cleveland Cavaliers three games to two in the best-of-five series. They advanced to the second round of the playoffs for the first time since 1981.

The Bulls' opponent in Round 2 was the Detroit Pistons, known as the bad boys of the NBA for their rough, defensive style of play. The Pistons were led by guards Isiah Thomas (who was behind Michael's freeze-out at the 1985 All-Star Game) and Joe Dumars, center Bill Laimbeer, and forward Dennis Rodman.

Detroit's coach, Chuck Daly, devised a special defense, called the "Jordan Rules," after Jordan burned the Pistons for 59 points in April 1988.

Michael holds up his 1988 MVP trophy at the All-Star Game in Chicago. (Associated Press)

"The Jordan Rules were a set of defensive principles the Pistons applied to stop me," Jordan later wrote in his book. "As far as I could tell, the plan involved running as many players as possible at me whenever I touched the ball and then hitting me as hard as possible every time I took a shot. Some rules."

The Jordan Rules were effective enough to lower Jordan's scoring average from 36.3 against the Cavaliers in the first round to 27.4 in the second round. The Pistons won the best-of-seven series in five games.

More of the Same

The 1988–89 season was nearly a carbon copy of the previous season. Michael won his third consecutive NBA scoring title, averaging 32.5 points a game. He was named All-NBA first team and All-Defensive first team. The Bulls' regular season win total declined slightly, from 50 to 47, but they qualified for the playoffs and advanced all the way to the Eastern Conference finals.

In the first round, they faced the Cavaliers, who had won all five regular season games against the Bulls and were favored to win the playoff series. Leading two games to one, the Bulls had a chance to close out the series at home, but failed to do so, when Michael missed a free throw and then a potential game-winner. Game 5 was played in Cleveland and it came down to the final second.

With three seconds to play and the Bulls trailing by one point, Jordan got the inbounds pass dribbled to the top of the key and let fly with a 20-footer over Craig Ehlo. "The Shot," as it has come to be known, swished through the hoop at the buzzer, sending the Bulls on to the Eastern Conference semifinals.

"If you accept the expectations of others, especially neg-ative expectations, then you never will change the out-come," Jordan wrote. "I believed no one could determine or dictate the result of the game I was playing. In Cleve-land, none of us believed we were going to lose, despite the records. We could determine the outcome. That was the attitude I had ever since I was cut from the varsity team in high school. That attitude became a part of me. I can't be successful without that approach."

In the next round, the Bulls faced the New York Knicks, who had the homecourt advantage because of their better record in the regular season. But the Bulls won the opener in Madison Square Garden in overtime, then closed out the series in Game 6 with another road win.

For the first time in team history, the Bulls had advanced to the Eastern Conference finals and another confrontation with the Detroit Pistons. The Pistons won the best-of-seven series in six games and went on to claim their first NBA championship.

Although Jordan did not get a championship ring in 1989, he did get a wedding ring. In September of that year, he married Juanita Vanoy, whom he had met during his second season in Chicago.

As for that elusive championship, Jordan and the Bulls would continue their quest for a title under a new coach. Doug Collins, who had been the Bulls coach since May

Juanita and Michael Jordan (Landov)

1986, was fired in July 1989. His replacement was Phil Jackson, who played for the New York Knicks in the late 1960s through the mid-1970s, but who had no experience as a head coach in the NBA.

The Zen Master

Coach Jackson practiced a Zen Buddhist philosophy, which brought calmness to the Bulls. This stood in contrast to Collins's emotional coaching style. Jackson taught the players to find peace within and to remain clear-headed in difficult moments. Jordan and the Bulls bought into Jackson's style.

Along with his Zen Buddhist mentality, Jackson also brought a new offensive system: the Triangle. The Triangle emphasized player movement and resulted in every player on the floor being a potential scoring option. It made it more difficult for opponents to double-team Jordan, which made him more dangerous.

One game that season was particularly memorable: March 28, 1990, at The Coliseum against the Cleveland Cavaliers. Early in the game, Jordan was knocked to the court by John "Hot Rod" Williams. While Jordan was down for a minute or two, the Cleveland fans cheered, which qualifies as bad sportsmanship in any league. Jordan decided to get even the only way he knew how: by scoring and scoring and scoring. When the game ended, the Bulls had won 117-113 in overtime, and Jordan had totaled a career-high 69 points.

Chicago finished the regular season with 55 wins, the second-highest total in the team's history, led by Jordan, of course, who won his fourth straight scoring title (33.6 points a game) and who led the league in steals (2.77).

The Bulls breezed through the first two rounds of the playoffs, beating the Milwaukee Bucks and the Philadelphia 76ers, losing just one game in each series. In their second straight trip to the Eastern Conference finals, the

Bulls coach Phil Jackson and Michael in 1996. Jackson taught his team to find peace within and to remain calm during difficult moments. (Associated Press)

Bulls met the defending NBA champion and their nemesis, the Detroit Pistons.

The outcome was the same, with the Pistons winning the series and going on to win their second straight NBA championship. But this time, the Bulls extended Detroit to the limit. After dropping the first two games, the Bulls won two straight to tie it. They eventually lost the deciding game.

"We lost in seven games, but Detroit had to know it couldn't hold us off again," Jordan wrote in *For the Love of the Game.* "We had the players, we had the system, and, after 1990, we had the confidence. I knew our time was coming and I knew we never would lose to the Pistons again, or anyone else for that matter, when it counted."

As it turned out, that was a prediction you could have taken to the bank.

5

THREEPEAT

The Bulls began the 1990–91 season with a veteran cast and high hopes. But the start was not what they expected. The Bulls lost their first three games, two of which were at home. That losing streak was the team's longest of the season.

Champions

Developing more continuity and confidence, the Bulls roared through the regular season with a team record 61 victories, including 26 straight at Chicago Stadium, their home court. They entered the postseason with the second-best record in the league.

Jordan averaged 31.5 points a game to win his fifth straight scoring title. He also made the All-Defensive first team for the fourth consecutive year and won his second NBA MVP Award.

The Bulls entered the playoffs with high expectations and had little trouble reaching the Eastern Conference finals for the third straight year. They defeated the New York Knicks in the first round and the Philadelphia 76ers in the second. Their opponent in the conference finals was none other than the two-time defending champion Detroit Pistons.

Although the matchup was the same, the result was drastically different. The Bulls won the best-of-seven series in four games and advanced to the NBA Finals against the Los Angeles Lakers, the team with legendary player Magic Johnson. The confrontation between Johnson and Jordan was highly anticipated.

Jordan got the best of the matchup, averaging 31.2 points, nearly twice as many as Johnson, and the Bulls got the best of the Lakers. The teams split the first two games in Chicago, but the Bulls closed out the series with three straight victories, winning their first NBA championship.

Sports Illustrated called Jordan's performance in the series "probably the finest all-around performance in a five-game Finals series." He was named MVP of the Finals by a unanimous vote. After the game in the locker room, he cradled the championship trophy the way a mother cradles a newborn. It meant that much to him.

In Jordan's mind, one of the most important things about winning a championship was the credibility it gave his career.

"I think people will now feel it's OK to put me in the category of players like Magic," Jordan told *Sports Illustrated.* "Personally, I always felt that in terms of intensity and unselfishness, I played like those type of players. Some people saw that, but many others didn't. And the championship, in the minds of a lot of people is a sign of, well, greatness. I guess they can say that about me now."

Problems off the Court

The 1991–92 season brought several non-basketball issues that Jordan had to deal with. Before the season even started, he caused some controversy by failing to join the rest of the team on a visit to the White House to meet President George H. W. Bush. Some people thought this was disrespectful behavior. But Jordan opted to spend the day with his family, which the Bulls gave him permission to do.

About a month later, Jordan and the rest of the sports world were shocked by Magic Johnson's announcement that he would be retiring from basketball because he was HIV-positive. Jordan was returning home from practice when he got a call from Johnson. The news so stunned Michael that he had to pull off the road and compose himself.

The most potentially damaging situation for Jordan occurred in March 1992, when three checks with Jordan's name on them and totaling $108,000 were found in the briefcase of a murdered man. There had been many rumors about Michael gambling, but these checks provided concrete evidence about the extent of his gambling. Fortunately for Jordan, an NBA investigation determined that no league rules had been broken, so he was not suspended or punished. In addressing his gambling, Jordan made no excuses.

"The gambling stories were situations I put myself in and I was responsible for my actions," Michael later said. ". . . I made a mistake and I faced the heat."

One More Time

On the court, the Bulls were enjoying another terrific season in 1991–92. At the halfway point, they were 37-5 and on pace to break the Los Angeles Lakers' record of 69 victories. They fell two wins short, however, finishing 67-15 and in first place in the Central Division.

Jordan averaged 30.1 points a game to win his sixth straight scoring title. He also won his third MVP Award and was named to the All-NBA first team and the All-Defensive first team.

But the postseason is where Jordan knew he could continue to make his mark. The Bulls, going for a second straight title, swept the Miami Heat in the first round, won a seventh game to defeat the New York Knicks in the

Eastern Conference semifinals, and then advanced to the NBA Finals after eliminating the Cleveland Cavaliers in six games in the Eastern Conference finals.

The Bulls faced the Portland Trail Blazers in the Finals, which meant a matchup between Jordan and Clyde Drexler, one of the most talented offensive players in the league. Drexler was looking to validate his career by going against—and defeating—Jordan, the way Jordan did the previous year in the Finals against Magic Johnson.

But it did not work out for Drexler the way it did for Jordan. In the much-anticipated face-off, Jordan dominated, averaging 35.8 points to Drexler's 24.8. The Bulls opened in Chicago Stadium with a 33-point rout in which Jordan had 35 points at the half and made six of his nine 3-point attempts, including five in a row.

The Trail Blazers evened the series, winning Game 2 in overtime; then the Bulls went up three games to two by winning two of the three games in Portland. Game 6 was back in Chicago Stadium and it looked as if a Game 7 would be a certainty. The Trail Blazers led 50-44 at the half and 79-64 after three quarters. After the game, Jordan admitted that as he sat on the bench at the start of the fourth period, he did not think a comeback was possible. But the combination of the Bulls' increased intensity and the Trail Blazers' turnovers and questionable shot selection helped the Bulls rally for a 97-93 victory. Jordan and

Scottie Pippen combined to score the team's final 19 points.

The Bulls had won their second NBA championship in a row, and Jordan proved once and for all that he was a team player who was not only good on his own, but who made those players around him better. But despite having proven this, he was not ready to rest on his laurels.

The Dream Team

Before the Chicago Bulls would set out to win their third straight NBA championship, Michael Jordan had another commitment: the 1992 Olympics in Barcelona, Spain. For the first time, the U.S. Olympic basketball team would be made up of NBA players, not college players. At first, Jordan was not sure he wanted to join the team. After all, he had already been on a gold medal-winning Olympic team in 1984 and thought someone else deserved the opportunity. But the lure of being a teammate of Magic Johnson (who had come out of retirement to take part in the Olympics), Larry Bird, and Charles Barkley, among others, convinced him to join what was becoming known as the Dream Team.

Not surprisingly, given the considerable talent on the U.S. team, the games were not very competitive. The Americans were not seriously challenged in any of their eight Olympic matchups. Because there were so many

Michael sails above teammate Magic Johnson during the
Summer Olympic Games in Barcelona, Spain, in 1992.
(Associated Press)

great players on the team, Jordan was more concerned with defense, rebounding, and making sure the other players on the court were involved in the offense. The result was one of the most dominant teams ever put together.

But the victory in the gold medal game left Jordan with a problem. Since his first year in the NBA, he had endorsed Nike products, but the sponsor of USA Basketball, which selected the Olympic team, was Reebok, one of Nike's rivals. Jordan did not want to appear on the medal stand wearing a Reebok product, but those refusing to wear the Reebok warmup suit could not take part in the ceremony. About 20 minutes before the ceremony was to start, Jordan came up with the solution: He got an American flag and draped it over the Reebok logo.

Michael Jordan left Barcelona with his second Olympic gold medal, to go along with an NCAA championship and two NBA championships. The quest for three in a row began almost immediately.

Back to Business

The Bulls' goal in the 1992–93 season was to *threepeat,* that is, win three straight NBA titles, which no team had done since the Boston Celtics won eight straight, starting in 1959. But Michael Jordan and Scottie Pippen began training camp, still tired from their Olympic experience. As a result, Coach Phil Jackson required them to practice just once a day—a decision that upset other players on the team who regarded it as a double standard.

But in spite of the unrest, the Bulls played well, finishing first in the Central Division with a 57-25 record. The first two rounds of the playoffs were a breeze. The Bulls swept the Atlanta Hawks in three games and the Cleveland Cavaliers in four to advance to the Eastern Conference finals against the New York Knicks.

The Knicks were a team that relied on their defense, which was spearheaded by Patrick Ewing, a 7'0" center. That defense, combined with the homecourt advantage of playing in Madison Square Garden, helped the Knicks win the first two games of the series: 98-90 in Game 1, 96-91 in Game 2.

The big story to come out of Game 2 was a newspaper report, alleging that Jordan spent the night before the game in an Atlantic City casino, where he stayed until the wee hours of the morning. Jordan admitted he was at the casino, but insisted he had returned to his hotel by midnight.

Although Michael was annoyed by the inaccurate report, he did not lash out in the press. Instead, he did it on the court, leading the Bulls to four straight victories, including a 105-95 win in Game 4 in which he scored 54 points. For the third straight year, the Bulls had advanced to the NBA Finals.

Dimming the Suns

The Bulls were on the verge of a monumental achievement. Most importantly for Jordan, it would allow him to accomplish what Magic Johnson and Larry Bird never did—three straight NBA titles.

The Bulls' opponent was the Phoenix Suns, who had the best record in the NBA and were led by Charles Barkley, a high-scoring, tough-rebounding forward who was known as much for his outspokenness as his basketball talent. Barkley was named the league's MVP, and he and Jordan were also good friends.

Jordan, though, was on a mission. After the first two games, both Bulls wins and both played in Phoenix, it looked as if the threepeat would come easily, since the next three games were set for Chicago. But the Suns proved their resilience by winning Game 3 in triple overtime. The Bulls won Game 4 to take a 3-1 lead, but the Suns proved their mettle by taking Game 5.

The series headed back to Phoenix, with the Bulls needing one victory to clinch it. With 14 seconds to play, the Bulls trailed by two points, 98-96. The plan was to get the ball to Jordan for the final shot, but the Suns double-teamed him. Seeing Jordan was covered, Horace Grant passed to John Paxson, who was stationed just beyond the 3-point line. Paxson took a shot that "I've taken hundreds of thousands of times" and watched it swish cleanly through the hoop, with 3.9 seconds to play. The Bulls led 99-98.

The Suns had one more chance to extend the series, but Grant blocked the shot of Kevin Johnson. The Bulls had completed their threepeat.

Again, Jordan dominated the matchup against the opponent's star player. He averaged 41 points to Barkley's 27.3 in the Finals and was voted the MVP of the series. He was also named to the All-NBA first team and the All-Defensive first team. He won his seventh consecutive scoring title, averaging 32.6 points a game, and tied Wilt Chamberlain for the most consecutive scoring titles.

But what had been a storybook run for Jordan the last three seasons was about to end, something only three people were aware of.

A Shock and Good-bye

Michael Jordan began thinking about retiring from the NBA as early as the 1992 Olympics. He admitted that the only reason he came back was to win that third NBA championship. He had accomplished all there was to accomplish with the Bulls, and he was tired and mentally drained from the stress of nearly two years of nonstop basketball, including the Olympics.

Jordan had discussed leaving the game with his father, James, and with his college coach, Dean Smith.

"By the time the 1993 playoffs started, I had made up my mind," Jordan wrote. "It was the perfect time. I knew it, my father knew it and Dean knew it. No one else had a clue."

But before Jordan could make his announcement, tragedy struck. On August 3, 1993, James Jordan was found murdered in a creek in South Carolina, just over the North Carolina border. James had gone to visit friends and was expected to be away for a few days. When his family did not hear from him for a week, the North Carolina state police were informed. Michael came home to North Carolina, hoping for the best, but it was not long before he learned the worst.

His father's car, a Lexus 400 that Michael bought for him, was found, abandoned, along a highway. A few days later, James's body was discovered in a creek. The investigation showed that he had been attacked by two 18-year-old boys and shot with a .38 pistol.

Michael had lost not only his father, but also the man he called his best friend. One of the lessons Jordan learned from his father was that everything happens for a reason. He used the experience of his father's death as, "God telling me it was time to stand up and make decisions by myself."

"I know he's with me," Jordan wrote. "I have all the life lessons and teachings he provided me in the 30 years I was around him. And I have his voice, his presence."

The aftermath of his father's death was a difficult time for Michael. But in his grief, he came to realize how precious life was. That realization, combined with the lack of challenges presented by his NBA career, made him follow through on his decision to retire. The announcement came October 6, 1993. Michael Jordan, the best player in the NBA and one of the greatest of all time, was retiring from the game he had dominated. He was 30 years old.

6

A WHOLE NEW BALLGAME

Michael and his father always talked baseball. It was one of their favorite topics of conversation. Even though Jordan had become a perennial all-star with the Chicago Bulls, James Jordan continued to think that his son could also play baseball. After all, there were other star athletes who had played two sports. Bo Jackson and Deion Sanders each played in the National Football League and Major League Baseball.

Although Jordan and his father had discussions about him playing baseball as far back as 1991, there was never enough time to pursue the possibility of taking a shot at baseball. Now that he was retired from basketball, he had all the time he needed, and Jerry Reinsdorf gave him the opportunity.

In addition to owning the Chicago Bulls, Reinsdorf also owned the Chicago White Sox, a team in the American

League. Jordan asked Reinsdorf for the chance to try out with the White Sox.

Jordan began working out in private, in order to keep the media away, with Bill Melton, a former member of the White Sox, and Herb Schneider, the team's trainer. The news finally leaked after about eight weeks. Jordan made it official in January 1994, announcing that he was going to try and make the White Sox roster.

From the Court to the Field

Jordan applied the same fervor, dedication, and work ethic to baseball that he did to basketball. He was determined to succeed, and there was much to learn: dealing with various hitting situations, learning how to hit a curveball and a slider, understanding how to run the bases, familiarizing himself with the many nuances of the game.

At spring training in Florida, he got to the ballpark at 6:00 A.M. to work for an hour or two with a hitting coach. Then he would go through the entire workout with the rest of the players; his day would end with another session with his hitting coach.

Despite his hard work, Jordan was having difficulty, especially at the plate. In 20 at-bats during exhibition games, he got only three hits. His dreams of bypassing the minor leagues and going right to the White Sox were not realized. Jordan was sent to Alabama to play for the

Birmingham Barons, a White Sox farm team in the Class AA Southern League. The highest classification of minor league baseball is Class AAA.

Even though Jordan was older than his teammates, everyone got along. They wanted to know all there was to know about Michael Jordan; he wanted to learn all he could from them about baseball. Jordan called it "one of the best times" of his life.

After a fast start, which included a 13-game hitting streak, Jordan tailed off. By the end of July, his average had fallen to .193, which is considered very low. But over the last month of the season, he hit .259, which raised his overall average to .202. He had three home runs, 51 runs batted in (RBIs), and 30 stolen bases. He was one of only five players in the Southern League that season to have done that.

End of the Line

Besides Michael Jordan playing for the Birmingham Barons, the other major baseball story in 1994 was a players' strike that shut down the game and led to the cancellation of the World Series. When spring training rolled around in 1995, the dispute still had not been settled, and major league teams were planning to start the exhibition season using replacement players. The White Sox asked Jordan to be one of those replacements.

Michael takes a swing for the Chicago White Sox during his one season as a professional baseball player. (Associated Press)

The request put Jordan in a difficult spot. He only wanted to make it to the major leagues on his own merits. Also, serving as a replacement player would not have put him in good standing with the striking major league players, many of whom on the White Sox he had befriended. To take part in the exhibition games was the same as crossing a picket line. Rather than help the owners, Jordan decided to call it quits, ending his baseball career after one season.

"I'm back."

With Jordan now retired yet again, people wondered whether he would return to the NBA. But when the season began in October 1994, he was not a member of the Chicago Bulls. It would not be long, however, before that changed.

At first Michael Jordan visited the Bulls at the Berto Center, their practice facility in Deerfield, a suburb of Chicago. Now and then he took the court during workouts. Eventually, he began practicing on a more regular basis. It was then that the rumors of his comeback began to circulate. But Jordan did nothing to verify those rumors. Because he refused to speak to the media about his plans, one member of the press took measures to force Jordan to make a statement.

The reporter disabled an electronic gate in the parking lot, so that Jordan would have to stop and open the gate manually when he arrived for practice. Jordan got word of the plan and had someone from the Bulls wait at the gate to open it when he arrived.

The news everyone was waiting to hear came Saturday, March 18. Jordan issued a two-word statement, which read, "I'm back." His first game would be the following afternoon at Market Square Arena in Indianapolis against the Indiana Pacers. NBC, which had already planned on airing the game live to 53 percent of the United States, expanded its coverage from coast to coast. It turned out to be the network's most watched NBA regular season telecast in five years.

Jordan was greeted by a thunderous ovation from the Pacers fans, who noticed one significant difference: His familiar number 23 had been replaced by 45. Jordan decided that he did not want to return to the game wearing the same number that his late father had seen him wear. So he chose number 45, because he had worn it in high school, as a basketball player and a baseball player. He also wore number 45 during his season in the White Sox organization.

The first game of Jordan's second career in the NBA was a mixed bag. He played 43 minutes and helped the Bulls rally from a 16-point fourth-quarter deficit and force the game into overtime. But he made only seven of his 28 field goal attempts, scoring 19 points. He found it difficult to get into a good rhythm with his teammates. The other thing that plagued Jordan was his conditioning: He was worn out by the second half. He had kept himself in shape while away from basketball, but he was not in game shape. That would take a bit of time to correct, but not too much time.

In his second game back, against the Boston Celtics, Jordan led the Bulls with 27 points. Two games later, he scored a game-high 32 points and made a shot at the buzzer to beat the Atlanta Hawks 99-98. This was the Michael Jordan everyone remembered.

In his fifth game back Jordan proved to everyone that he had not lost any of his magic during his time away. The Bulls traveled to New York's Madison Square Garden for a game against the Knicks, a strong defensive team and one of the Bulls' fiercest rivals. Any time Jordan played in New York was big news, but this was something special, particularly for Jordan, who played as if he never left the game. He scored 55 points—a "double nickel," as he called it—and led the Bulls to 113-111 victory.

"I think the fact the game was in Madison Square Garden had something to do with my performance," Jordan wrote. "I always wanted to play well in New York, because it's a basketball Mecca."

Jordan returned to the Bulls with 17 games to play in the regular season. The Bulls won 13 and qualified for the playoffs with a 47-35 record. In the first round, they defeated the Charlotte Hornets three games to one. They then advanced to the Eastern Conference semifinals to meet the Orlando Magic, the conference champions led by 7'1" center Shaquille O'Neal.

Jordan had a chance to win the first game of the series in the final seconds, but as he was heading downcourt, Orlando's Nick Anderson stole the ball and the Magic went on to win.

After the game, Anderson commented that 45, Jordan's new number, did not have the same quickness that 23 had. Jordan was miffed enough by Anderson's remark that he went back to No. 23 for Game 2 of the series. The switch worked. Jordan scored 38 points and Chicago won to tie the series.

The teams alternated wins in Games 3 and 4, but the Magic closed out the Bulls by winning the final two games to move on to the NBA Finals, where they lost in four straight games to the Houston Rockets. It was the first time in Jordan's last five playoff series that the Bulls failed to reach the conference finals. But there was always next year; and next year, Jordan would be with the Bulls for the entire season.

In the Movies

Before Michael began thinking about the next basketball season, he had another commitment to fulfill: the lead role in *Space Jam,* a movie in which his costars were Bugs Bunny, Daffy Duck, Elmer Fudd, Sylvester and Tweety,

Speedy Gonzalez, Foghorn Leghorn and the rest of the Looney Tunes characters. The film also featured some other NBA players: Charles Barkley, Muggsy Bogues, Shawn Bradley, and Patrick Ewing. The mix of live action and animation proved to be a huge success. The film was one of the biggest hits of 1996, earning more than $90 million in the United States and more than $250 million worldwide.

Jordan's main concern about the filming was whether he would be able to work on his game. He told his agent, David Falk, that the only way he would be able to do the movie was if he were able to practice. So a gym was built

Jordan and costar Bugs Bunny in the 1996 film Space Jam (Photofest)

on the movie set, complete with air conditioning, stereo system, card tables, and weightlifting machines. Jordan lifted weights over lunch and played pick-up games from 7:00 to 9:30 every evening. Many NBA players, including Reggie Miller, Charles Oakley, Dennis Rodman, Juwan Howard, Rod Strickland, and Grant Hill, were frequent visitors.

Jordan figured the other NBA players showed up to learn about his game and how he was going to play. But he did the same thing.

"So they were helping me just like I was helping them," Jordan wrote. "I could feel it coming back pretty quickly."

7

THE ULTIMATE TEAM PLAYER

Michael Jordan entered the 1995–96 season eager to play and feeling he had something to prove. While he played well the previous season after returning to the Bulls, there were whispers that he was not quite the same player. Some people wondered whether he would be as explosive and effective as he was before he attempted to make it as a baseball player. So Jordan was even more motivated than usual to perform up to his high standards.

"I couldn't wait for the season to start," Jordan wrote. "I knew my game had come back with all the work I put in over the summer. I felt like a kid coming out of college with something to prove."

That season, Jordan and the Bulls proved to everyone that they were one of the greatest teams in NBA history.

They won 41 of their first 44 games, including 18 games in a row, and finished the season with the best record ever—72 wins, 10 losses.

Jordan scored 40 or more points nine times; his high game for the year was 53 points in a win over Detroit. He won his eighth scoring title, with an average of 30.4 points a game; was named to the All-Star team and the All-Defensive team; and earned the league's MVP Award for the fourth time.

The Bulls began the playoffs as the odds-on favorites to win. After their remarkable regular season, it was expected that they would win their fourth championship in six seasons. They did not disappoint.

Chicago stormed through the first three rounds of the playoffs by losing only one game. In the first round, they beat the Miami Heat three games to none in a best-of-five series, winning by an average margin of 23 points. The New York Knicks did not fare much better in the Eastern Conference semifinals, losing the best-of-seven series four games to one.

In the conference finals, the Bulls faced the Orlando Magic. A year earlier, the Magic eliminated the Bulls in four straight games. This year, though, the Bulls got their revenge, winning in a four-game sweep by an average margin of 18 points a game.

Four-Time Champs

Jordan and the Bulls had made it back to the NBA Finals, where their opponent was the Seattle SuperSonics. The SuperSonics, winners of the Western Conference title, were expected to be defeated without putting up much of a fight. For the first three games of the series, that's the way it looked. The Bulls took a three-games-to-none lead, but lost the next two games.

The fifth game was played in Chicago on Sunday, June 16, 1996, Father's Day. The Bulls went on to win the championship that day. This win was particularly significant for Jordan, not just because his team won the title and his comeback had been successful, but because winning on Father's Day was a tribute to his father.

After the game in the trainer's room, Jordan, named MVP in the Finals, lay on the floor and sobbed. The emotion of winning the championship and the loss of his father was almost too much to bear. But he could not have been happier about the way the season turned out.

"It couldn't have played out any better," Jordan wrote. "I was so determined that day. It was like sometimes you get so angry that you cry. That's how determined I was to win that game. I was so angry and so happy at the same time. There was no way I could control my emotions.

"I was angry because I felt like I had to win another championship before anyone would give credence to my return. But I was happy that I proved my point. I had loved the game for so long and done so much in the game and yet I was still being criticized. . . . There had been some disappointments along the way, but they [his parents] had taught me to do the right thing. If you do the work, you get rewarded. There are no shortcuts in life."

That is a lesson Jordan learned early on in life, when he was a young boy growing up in North Carolina, and even as he rose to become the best player of his era, he never lost sight of the value of hard work.

Taking the Fifth

Coming off a year in which they set the NBA regular season records for wins, the Bulls gave themselves a tough act to follow in the 1996–97 season. But they were up to the challenge. They opened the new season with a 12-game winning streak and went on to win 34 of their first 38 games. At the All-Star break, the Bulls were 42-6.

Jordan was named to the All-Star team for the 11th time and he made history by becoming the first player ever to record a triple-double (double digit scores in three statistical categories). He had 14 points, 11 rebounds, and 11 assists.

The Bulls continued to play well throughout the second half of the season, and Jordan led the team in scoring in almost every game. The Bulls did not equal their record-setting total of 72 wins, but they came close, finishing 69-13 and tying the 1971–72 Los Angeles Lakers for the second-best record of all time.

Jordan won his ninth scoring title, with an average of 29.6 points a game. He was also All-NBA and All-Defensive first team.

Once again the Bulls were the favorites to win the championship, and once again they breezed through the first three rounds of the playoffs. They swept the Washington Wizards in the first round and lost one game in each of the next two series, against the Atlanta Hawks and the Miami Heat.

Their opponent in the NBA Finals was the Utah Jazz, led by one of the most effective duos ever to play: point guard John Stockton and power forward Karl Malone. The Bulls, and Michael, especially, were up to the challenge. Many consider the series against Utah one of the best of Michael's career.

Jordan's magic was evident in Game 1, which was tightly contested throughout, with neither team able to pull away. With the clock winding down and the Jazz leading by one, Jordan drove to his left, stopped, and buried a 3-pointer at the buzzer to give the Bulls an 84-82 victory. Great players want the ball in tough situations when the game is on the line. Time and again during his career, Jordan was able to come through in the clutch.

Game 2 was more of Jordan doing what he does best. He scored 38 points as the Bulls won by 12. The series shifted to Utah for the next three games, and the Jazz took the first two to even the series. Then in Game 5, Jordan turned in what has to rank as one of his most remarkable performances. That he played at all in Game 5 on June 11, 1997, was unfathomable. That he played so spectacularly was a miracle.

Jordan's problem began at 3:00 A.M. the morning of the game, when he awoke with what he thought was stomach flu. The discomfort kept him awake, but knowing he needed his rest to play his best against the Jazz, he took something to help him sleep. Instead of making him drowsy, the medication made his flu symptoms worse. After spending the entire day in his hotel room, he left for the arena, exhausted and without having eaten. He tried drinking coffee, hoping that would give him a jolt, but it did not work.

By the time the game started, Jordan was not feeling any better. He had a fever and he was dehydrated. Said Scottie Pippen, "I didn't even think he would be able to put his uniform on."

Somehow, though, he managed. Jordan started the game and scored 19 points by halftime.

When he returned to the locker room at halftime, he was still dehydrated, and at times during the third and fourth quarters, Jordan felt as if he might pass out. But he persevered, somehow managing to draw strength from deep within himself; strength that most people do not possess.

He struggled through the third period, scoring just two points. But in the fourth quarter of a close game, Jordan turned in a Superman-like performance. He tied the game at 85 by making the first of two free throws; then after missing the second, came up with the rebound. With 25 seconds to play he made a 3-pointer that proved to be the game-winner.

"On the last shot, I didn't even know whether it went in or not," said Jordan, who scored 38 points, 15 in the fourth quarter alone, and played 44 minutes. "I could barely stand up. When I got back into the locker room the doctors were really concerned because I didn't have anything left. I was cold, yet I was sweating, dehydrated. They wanted to give me intravenous fluids, but I made it over to a table, lay down and started drinking Gatorade. That's all I did for about 45 minutes. All for a basketball game."

The Bulls returned to Chicago for Game 6 of the NBA Finals, and like most of the other games in the series, the outcome was in doubt until the final seconds. The Bulls did not play up to their usual standards and led for less than five minutes in the entire game. But it has often been said that the mark of a championship team is the ability to win when it is not playing its best. Such was the case with the Bulls in Game 6.

Surprisingly, though, the hero was not Jordan, it was Steve Kerr, a reserve guard. During a timeout immediately before the Bulls' last possession, Jordan, expecting to be double-teamed, warned Kerr to be ready. He was. He took a pass from Jordan and hit the game-winning jump shot with five seconds to play. Jordan was named MVP of the NBA Finals for the fifth time.

The Bulls' fifth NBA title prompted much discussion about where the team ranked with two of the greatest dynasties of all time: the Boston Celtics and Los Angeles Lakers. But while that debate raged, there were few who disagreed that Michael Jordan, once dismissed as a scorer and not much else, had become the ultimate team player.

Grand Finale

When the 1997–98 season began, there was some uncertainty about the future of the Chicago Bulls. The contracts of Michael Jordan and Scottie Pippen, the team's mainstays, and head coach Phil Jackson were set to expire at season's end. The team's top executives, owner Jerry Reinsdorf and general manager Jerry Krause, had always planned on rebuilding the team after the season, despite its success. Jordan had said repeatedly that he would not play for a coach other than Jackson, so there was a strong possibility that the season could be the last hurrah for Jordan and his teammates.

That feeling was shared by the rest of the players and coaching staff, who realized that this could be the end of their time together. They made the most of it. Their record was not quite as good as the past two seasons, but it was good enough. The Bulls finished 62-20 and set an NBA record for the most victories over a three-year span (203-43, .825 winning percentage).

Jordan, on his way to claiming his 10th NBA scoring title and his fifth MVP award, passed Hall-of-Fame member Moses Malone for third place on the NBA's all-time scoring list. In a December 30, 1997, game against the Minnesota Timberwolves, Jordan scored in double figures for the 788th time, passing former Los Angeles Lakers great Kareem Abdul Jabbar, who had held the mark at 787.

Realizing that his time remaining in a Bulls uniform could be ending, Michael commemorated what might have been his last visit to Madison Square Garden in New York in a special way. Before the team left for New York, Jordan's wife, Juanita, was doing some spring cleaning and found a pair of original Air Jordans in a closet. Jordan decided to wear the shoes as a statement of how he felt about the city and its fans. The rivalry with the Knicks was heated, but he always enjoyed playing on the game's biggest stage. No one knew about the shoes until he put them on in the locker room before the game. Even though they were a bit too tight, Jordan wore them and the fans appreciated the gesture, saluting Jordan after the game with a standing ovation—even though the Bulls beat the Knicks and Jordan scored 42 points.

The playoffs started out for the Bulls much the same as they had in the previous two years—easily. They breezed into the Eastern Conference finals by sweeping the New Jersey Nets three games to none and eliminating the Charlotte Hornets four games to one in the semifinals. But in the Eastern Conference finals, the Indiana Pacers extended the Bulls to a seventh game; something that happened only one other time during their previous five championships.

The Bulls won the first two games of the series, but the Pacers tied it by winning Games 3 and 4. In Game 4, Pacers guard Reggie Miller hit the game-winning basket over Jordan. The teams traded wins in Games 5 and 6, meaning the series came down to Game 7, which was at the United Center in Chicago.

The Bulls did not play all that well, and Jordan and Pippen did not shoot all that well. But the Bulls' strong rebounding, combined with their toughness on defense, allowed them to prevail 88-83.

Next stop was their sixth trip to the NBA Finals, and for the second time in their run of championships, the Bulls did not have the homecourt advantage. The Utah Jazz, champions of the Western Conference, earned the extra home game in the best-of-seven series. The Bulls and the Jazz finished the regular season with the same record, but the Jazz earned the advantage by winning both games against the Bulls during the regular season.

Except for Game 3, which Chicago won 96-54 (which was the largest margin of victory in Finals history), every game in the series was close. The Jazz won the opener in overtime by five points; the Bulls evened the series with a five-point win in Game 2. In Game 4, the Bulls won by four; in Game 5, the Jazz won by two and trailed three games to two in the series.

Game 6, played in Utah, followed the same route and was close from start to finish. With 41.9 seconds to play, Jazz guard John Stockton hit a 3-pointer for an 86-83 lead. Then Jordan took over with a three-play sequence that in many ways defines him as a player.

- Play number 1: After Stockton's 3-pointer, Jordan quickly got the ball downcourt and made a layup that brought the Bulls within a point. But most importantly, the play used only 4.8 seconds.
- Play number 2: With the Jazz looking to increase their lead, Jordan sneaked behind Karl Malone and stole the ball.

■ Play number 3: Jordan, who never gave up possession, brought the ball downcourt. Steve Kerr, who hit the game-winning shot in Game 6 of the 1997 Finals, was guarded by Stockton. Jordan was guarded by Byron Russell. Jordan stutter-stepped (a quick, short step used to fake out a defender), dribbled, and as soon as Russell lunged for the ball, Jordan let it fly from 17 feet. The shot was good from the moment it left his hand. Jordan held his follow-through position until the ball went through the hoop. If this was to be his final game with the Bulls, that freeze frame of the game-winning shot would be remembered forever.

There were still 5.2 seconds remaining after Jordan gave the Bulls the lead. But Stockton missed a 3-pointer on the Jazz's final possession; the Bulls had won their sixth NBA title, and Jordan his sixth NBA Finals MVP Award.

"When Russell reached, I took advantage of the moment," Jordan said. "I never doubted myself. I never doubted the whole game."

Jordan finished with 45 points in Game 6, and many believe that his performance exceeded last year's when he played so brilliantly, despite being so ill.

Jordan jams in a basket during the 1997–98 season. This would be his last season with the Chicago Bulls. (Landov)

"I didn't think he could top that game," Coach Phil Jackson said. "He topped it tonight. I think it was the best performance I've seen in a critical situation and critical game in a series."

Of course, the question that everyone wanted answered was whether Jordan would continue playing. But that answer would have to wait.

"If and when that time comes when I have to walk away, I hope no one will look at me and think any less," Jordan said. "I have another life I have to get to at some point in time. Hopefully, everyone will understand."

Asked if his game-winning shot in Game 6 would serve as a fitting way to go out, Jordan smiled and said, "If that's the case, yes."

8

ENDINGS AND BEGINNINGS

It was not long after the end of the 1998 NBA Finals that Michael Jordan put Bulls owner Jerry Reinsdorf on alert. Jordan told his boss he was seriously thinking about retiring. It was not that he was worn out physically; it was that he was exhausted mentally. In addition to that, he was out of challenges. He had led his team to six NBA championships, won 10 scoring titles, and been named MVP five times. He felt there was nothing left for him to accomplish.

Another major consideration in Jordan's decision-making was the Bulls' hiring of a new coach. Phil Jackson's contract was not renewed and the team hired Tim Floyd, who left Iowa State University to take the job in Chicago. Jordan likened playing for a coach other than Jackson to a child being assigned new parents.

"What would you want?" Jordan wrote in *For the Love of the Game.* "Would you want to stay with your original parents or with the new parents? The old parents were the people who taught you everything, fed you, helped you through certain periods of your life. Now they say you have to go through the same process with new parents?" That's how I feel about playing for another coach."

Farewell

Jordan's decision to retire was a secret between himself and his wife, Juanita—a secret that had to be kept for months. Jordan didn't announce his retirement until January 1999, because of a labor dispute involving NBA players and owners that canceled the first several months of the 1998–99 season. He wanted to be able to voice his opinions and stand up for his fellow players during the negotiations, and he might not have been as effective had he announced his retirement.

But once the dispute was settled, the question about Jordan's future was one everyone wanted answered. The word came on January 14 at a press conference at the United Center. Accompanied by Juanita and NBA commissioner David Stern, Jordan made it official: One month shy of his 36th birthday, he was retiring from basketball.

"It was difficult because you are giving up something that you truly, truly love," Jordan said at his farewell press conference. "My love for the game is very strong, and it's hard to give up that love. For the sake of the mental challenges that Michael Jordan needs to drive himself to be the best basketball player he can be, I don't want to fool myself going into the situation knowing that I am not 100 percent challenged mentally. Physically, I feel fine . . . Mentally, I just felt like I didn't have the challenges in front of me."

Asked if there was a chance he would change his mind sometime down the road, Jordan answered: "No, I never say never, but 99.9 percent I am very secure with my decision."

The Bulls had retired number 23 when Michael left to play baseball in 1993, but had removed it from the rafters when he returned to the NBA 16 months later. During his retirement announcement in 1999, Reinsdorf unveiled a banner of number 23, hanging from the rafters, as part of the ceremony. Reinsdorf called the occasion "a tough day for basketball fans all over the world," and "the day I had hoped would never come."

Stern praised Jordan for his contributions to the game, calling them "immeasurable."

"Thank you for gracing our court for 13 seasons," Stern said. "And I disagree with Jerry, this is not a sad day, this is a great day because the greatest basketball player in the history of the game is getting the opportunity to retire with the grace that described his play."

Given all he did for the NBA, on and off the court, Michael Jordan deserved nothing less.

The Next Chapter

When Michael announced his retirement, the press asked him about his plans for the future. What was one of the most competitive athletes, in any sport, going to do with his time?

Jordan insisted he would find plenty to do and that spending time with Juanita and their three children, Jeffrey, Marcus, and Jasmine, would be the highest priority. Juanita joked that she expected Michael would be doing more carpooling. In addition to family time, Jordan had many business interests to attend to, and he was an avid golfer, who was known to play 36 holes in one day.

But Jordan also talked about taking on different challenges. On January 19, 2000, nearly one year to the day after he retired from the Chicago Bulls, he took on one of those new challenges. Although this time, he would be wearing a suit instead of a uniform. Jordan was named president of basketball operations and part owner of the Washington Wizards of the NBA. He signed a five-year contract to help turn the Wizards, a struggling franchise that had not won a playoff game in 12 years, into a winner. Abe Pollin, the Wizards' majority owner, had been after Jordan for five months. Pollin believed that Jordan's drive,

Michael is an avid golfer. He has been known to play 36 holes a day. (Photofest)

determination, work ethic, and winning attitude on the court would translate to the front office.

"[Jordan] makes everybody better," Pollin said. "He's a fierce competitor. He will not accept losing. He's going to get the best out of everybody. And that's why I've turned the basketball operations over to him."

Jordan did not hide that he was inexperienced when it came to being an executive, but he also made it clear that he was eager to start working—and learning—at his new job, which included assembling the players on the team and deciding on the coach.

"This is new to me," said Jordan. "Being in charge is something that I never had an opportunity to do. Maybe that's not the ingredient that may turn this team around. Then again, it may be. That's the beauty of trying.

"I won't be wearing the Wizards' uniform. I have an attitude about the way I play. I have an attitude about the way I win, and my job and responsibility with this organization is to see if I can pass it on to the players in that uniform."

One-tenth of One Percent

Michael Jordan did not waste any time putting his stamp on the Washington Wizards. Twelve days after he was hired, he fired Garfield Heard, the Wizards head coach, and replaced him with Darrell Walker for the rest of the 1999–2000 season. The Wizards finished with a record of

29-53 and failed to make the playoffs for the third straight year.

Before the start of the next season, Jordan hired Leonard Hamilton, who had had success as a college coach at Oklahoma State and the University of Miami in Florida, to take over the Wizards. During the season, he also completed several trades to help the team get better players. But for the most part, the moves failed. The Wizards had another disappointing season. They finished with 10 fewer wins than in 1999–2000 and a record of 19-63, second-worst in franchise history.

Hamilton resigned after the season, and Jordan would have to hire the team's fourth coach since he took over as president of basketball operations. This time, Jordan chose Doug Collins, who was his coach with the Bulls from 1986 through 1989. Collins, an outstanding player with the Philadelphia 76ers, was experienced and well respected throughout the NBA.

About the time Jordan hired Collins, he also began working out—and with the workouts came the rumors that he was preparing to come out of retirement to play for the Wizards. But Jordan insisted that the only reason he was in training was to lose some of the extra weight he had gained since he retired.

The workouts became more intense, and Jordan got himself into playing shape by holding pickup games with other NBA players at a Chicago gym. But in spite of the speculation, there was no announcement that Jordan would return. Complicating the matter were several injuries Jordan suffered during the summer. He experienced back spasms, tendinitis in his knees, and two cracked ribs, sustained in a collision in a pickup game.

By the end of the summer, Jordan was healthy once again. On September 25, 2001, he made an announcement that had become the worst-kept secret in sports. About two and a half years earlier, Jordan made it clear that he would "never say never" about pursuing a comeback. He said he was "99.9 percent" sure he would remain retired, but he also gave himself the option of returning, by using that one-tenth of one percent.

Jordan called his return to the game "an itch that still needs to be scratched." He also said he did not want "that itch to bother [him] for the rest of his life."

"I am returning as a player to the game I love," he said.

There were some people who thought Jordan should have stayed retired; they feared that a comeback after more than three years away from the game might tarnish his legacy, because at age 38, many doubted he could be the Michael Jordan that everyone remembered. Many also thought that retiring after hitting the winning shot in the title-clinching game against Utah was the perfect way to end his brilliant career.

But Jordan took the advice of Mario Lemieux, the superstar player for the Pittsburgh Penguins hockey team, who left the game and then made a successful comeback. Lemieux told Jordan that if he truly wanted to return to the NBA, then he owed it to himself to do it.

Jordan made it clear he was not worried that there were people who doubted him; nor was he overly concerned about failing to live up to the expectations of others. He was coming back to the NBA because he believed he could still be a productive player and because his love of the game had not waned during his time away.

"I'm not walking into this scenario thinking I'm failing," Jordan said at the press conference to announce his return. "I'm walking in thinking I'm confident and I'm pretty sure that I can make it work. If I sit here and listened to everyone else tell me that I can't do it, then obviously I wouldn't be here.

"When I left the game, I left something on the floor. . . . I'm not walking into the dark. I know what I'm capable of doing. I know what's going to be expected of me. I know everybody is putting my head on the chopping block."

But for Jordan, the prospect of trying and not doing as well as he expected was a better alternative than not trying at all.

In order to become a member of the Wizards, Jordan had to resign his position as president of basketball operations. He also had to sell his minority ownership in the team.

Jordan, who earned $33 million in his last year playing for the Chicago Bulls, was paid $1.03 million, the minimum salary for a 10-year veteran in the NBA. He was the lowest-paid player on his team. But for Jordan, it was not about the money, it was about the competition, and about the challenge of coming back and playing the game he loved. To prove it was not about the money, he donated his entire first-year salary to help the victims of the September 11, 2001, terrorist attacks.

9

BACK IN
THE GAME

Doug Collins, Washington Wizards coach, was in an enviable and difficult position. What coach would not want Michael Jordan on his team? Even at the relatively advanced age of 38 and having been away from the game for more than three years, Jordan was still one of the better players in the league. His personal pride and determination would not allow for anything less.

But Collins was now coaching the executive that hired him. Would he be able to determine the amount of time Jordan played? Or would Jordan make the call as to how much and when he played?

As it turned out, Collins began the season wanting to limit the number of minutes Jordan played in order to reduce the wear and tear on the player's body. Collins even considered using Jordan as a reserve. But neither alternative occurred, because of Jordan's desire to help his team win.

Jordan, who expected to resume his front office duties after his playing days were finished, wanted to set an example and send a message to the rest of the members of the team, many of whom were young players. He was playing in the present, but building toward the future. He could not do that while sitting on the bench.

Brand New Start

The Wizards began their season at one of Jordan's favorite arenas—Madison Square Garden. Jordan took the court for the Wizards playing a different position than he played for the Bulls. Instead of being a shooting guard, he had been switched to the small forward position, which would mean less ball-handling responsibilities.

While many were hoping for a spectacular performance, Jordan turned in one that was solid on his first night back. He played 37 minutes and had 19 points, five rebounds, six assists and four steals in a 93-91 loss to the Knicks.

As you might expect, Jordan was not the same player as he was with the Bulls. In spite of his greatness, not even Jordan was able to stop the passage of time and the aging process. He was not as quick or explosive as he was prior to retiring in 1999. But what he lacked physically he made up for mentally. His knowledge of the game that he acquired over the years served him well. His mental toughness allowed him to compete with players who were years younger.

There were times during the season that Jordan made it seem as if no time at all had passed. Through the first 26 games of the season, he scored 30 or more points eight times, including a 44-point effort against the Utah Jazz. But on December 27, 2001, in a game against the Indiana Pacers, Jordan made only two of 10 shots and scored a career-low six points.

It was not long before Jordan redeemed himself. In the team's next game, two nights later, the Wizards played the Charlotte Hornets, who saw number 23 at his best. Jordan scored a season-high 51 points in an easy win for the Wizards, and in doing so, became the oldest NBA player ever to score 50 points in a game.

Said Jordan afterward, "After tonight, I'm pretty sure people are going to say that I can still play this game."

They said the same thing the next night, when Jordan scored 45 points in a victory over the New Jersey Nets.

In January 2002, ironically enough in a game against the Chicago Bulls, Jordan surpassed the 30,000-point mark. Jordan not only reached a career milestone, but he also demonstrated he still had a flair for the dramatic. Jordan hit a 15-footer at the buzzer to lift the Wizards to a one-point victory over the Cleveland Cavaliers, and a few weeks later, he did the same thing to the Phoenix Suns, scoring with 0.2 seconds left.

Wounded Knee

Jordan had problems with his right knee for most of the 2001–02 season. Inflammation caused him to miss a game in early December 2001, and he had the knee drained of fluid five times during the season. He bruised it in February 2002, forcing him to miss another game, but he came right back and played three games in four days. Those games turned out to be the last he would play for nearly a month. He underwent arthroscopic surgery on his knee and was placed on the injured list. He was out for 12 games.

Jordan was back in the lineup March 20, 2002, even though his knee was only "65 percent," according to Collins. The reason he came back so quickly was to help the Wizards make the playoffs. But by necessity, Jordan's role was reduced. His playing time was reduced to between 20 and 28 minutes a game, whereas before, he had been averaging about 37 minutes a game. But after playing just two minutes against the Los Angeles Lakers on April 2, 2002, the team placed Jordan on the injured list and he missed the final eight games of the season.

The Wizards finished with a record of 37-45, an 18-game improvement over the previous year. That was good, but not good enough to achieve Jordan's goal of making the playoffs. They were within two games of the final Eastern Conference playoffs when he went on the injured list for the second time. Without Michael, the Wizards were unable to qualify.

For the season, Jordan led the team in scoring with an average of 22.9 points a game. He averaged 34.9 minutes, 5.7 rebounds, 5.2 assists and 1.4 steals. He also proved to be one of the NBA's most popular attractions—yet again. The Wizards sold out every home game, and they played to sold-out crowds on the road in every game but one.

Now the question was, would Michael Jordan return for a second season in Washington?

Return Engagement

When Michael Jordan stepped down as president of basketball operations for the Washington Wizards, he signed a two-year contract worth $2.2 million. But whether he would be willing or able to fulfill the deal was uncertain. With 11 games to play in the 2001–02 season, Coach Doug Collins candidly said he would be surprised if Jordan played another season. Jordan had said all along that he planned to play for another season, but the condition of his knee and whether he would be able to endure another 82-game season had not been determined.

In the offseason, Jordan said that if his right knee was not healthy enough, he would not play. But ultimately, he decided he was physically fit enough to return for a second season with the Wizards—for one more year. He left no doubt that his next retirement would be final, saying there was "zero chance" he would play again.

"It's about that time," he said. "That itch is about to be completed. I just want to fulfill my year and enjoy it. From that point, I'll move on."

Collins again planned on limiting Jordan's playing time and again suggested that he might be used off the bench. Jordan responded, "No decisions have been made as to my exact role on the team."

Jordan appeared in each of the 82 regular season games in 2002–03, and he started 67, which said as much as anything did about his physical condition. It is rare for an athlete to play such a big part in every game—offensively and defensively—and miss so few games.

Collins managed to use Jordan sparingly during the first 10 games. Only once did Jordan play as many as 30 minutes. But most of the rest of the season, his minutes played were consistently in the mid-30s, and often over 40, including a 53-minute stint in a victory over Indiana in which he scored 41 points, just four off his season high. That game was arguably the best he ever played for the

Wizards. In addition to the 41 points, he also had 12 rebounds, four assists and three steals in a double-overtime victory.

Brightest Star

One of the highlights of the season for Michael was being named to the NBA All-Star team for the 14th time. The game was as much a farewell to Jordan as it was a showcase for the league's best players. From the start, everything was geared toward giving Jordan a fitting sendoff.

Jordan, who was not on the team as a starter for the Eastern Conference, ended up starting, because Vince Carter of the Toronto Raptors relinquished his spot as a tribute to Jordan. At halftime, the league honored Jordan with an emotional ceremony that included a performance by singer Mariah Carey. Jordan, who was visibly moved by the ceremony and outpouring from the crowd, said, "I thank you for your support; I leave the game in good hands."

The game nearly turned out to be worthy of a Hollywood scriptwriter. With 4.8 seconds to play in overtime, Jordan got the ball along the right baseline and hit a fadeaway jumper (a jump shot taken while falling away from the basket) to give the East a 138-136 lead. It looked as if Jordan's final All-Star game would end with yet another game-winning shot. But Jermaine O'Neal of the Indiana

Pacers was called for a foul on Kobe Bryant of the Los Angeles Lakers. Bryant made both free throws and the West went on to win in the second overtime, ruining what would have been a storybook finish.

Two weeks after the All-Star game, Jordan turned in another vintage performance against the New Jersey Nets. He had 43 points in 43 minutes in a victory that was crucial to the Wizards' playoff hopes. Jordan became the first player his age, 40, to score more than 40 points in a game.

As the season wound down and Jordan's career as a player neared an end, the tributes began. At his third-to-last-game, in Miami, that city's team, the Heat, took the unusual step of retiring Jordan's No. 23.

Said Miami coach Pat Riley: "In honor of your greatness and for all you've done for the game of basketball—and not just the NBA, but for fans all around the world—we want to honor you tonight and hang your No. 23 jersey from the rafters. No one will ever wear No. 23 for the Miami Heat again. You're the best."

The gesture took Jordan by surprise. He called it "by far, the best gift I ever could have received."

Jordan's final game took place on April 16, 2003, in Philadelphia against the 76ers, who gave him a sendoff that was worthy of the honoree. Before the game, Jordan, an avid golfer, was presented with a golf cart, driven onto the court by former Sixers players and basketball Hall of Fame members Julius "Dr. J" Erving and Moses Malone.

When it came time for the pregame introductions, Jordan, who was introduced last, was brought onto the court by a familiar voice. As a surprise to Jordan, the team had Ray Clay, the announcer for the Chicago Bulls, to introduce Jordan one last time, in signature fashion: "From North Carolina . . . 6-6 . . . No. 23 . . . Michael Jordan." The standing ovation from the Philadelphia fans lasted for three minutes.

The Wizards were routed in Jordan's final game. The Sixers won by 20 points. Because the score was so lopsided, Jordan left the game—apparently for good—with 4:35 to play. But the fans began chanting, "We want Mike; we want Mike." Jordan, who complained of stiffness, heard the fans but did not want to return, despite the urging from his coach, Doug Collins. Finally, after some more prodding by Collins, Jordan pulled off his warmup suit and entered the game with 2:35 to play.

A short time later, Sixers guard Eric Snow, on instructions from his coach, Larry Brown, fouled Jordan, sending him to the foul line. Jordan made both free throws and then left the court for the final time to another prolonged standing ovation. In a rare display of respect, the 10 players on the court applauded along with the rest of the fans.

"Now I guess it hits me that I'm not going to be in a uniform anymore—and that's not a terrible feeling," Jordan said. "It's something that I've come to grips with, and it's time. This is the final retirement."

Jordan finished his final season, averaging 37 minutes, 20 points, six rebounds, 3.8 assists, and 1.50 steals a game. Despite playing on a problematic knee, his average minutes per game in his final season was only slightly more than a minute less than his average minutes per game for his career.

Obviously, Jordan was not the same player physically as he had been with the Bulls, but the passion and heart with which he played the game was still strong.

"I never, never took the game for granted," Jordan said. "I was very true to the game, and the game was very true to me. It was just that simple."

Next Steps

In the final days of Michael Jordan's career as a player with the Washington Wizards, he began planning how he might build the Wizards into a playoff contender by returning to his position as president of basketball operations. After two years of playing for the Wizards, Jordan had a chance to evaluate the players on his team and those on other teams. He knew what the Wizards needed, and he wanted to build the team accordingly when he returned to the front office.

Michael waves to the crowd after scoring the final point of his career. (Landov)

But before he had a chance to put his plan in place, Wizards owner Abe Pollin shocked Jordan—and the sports world—by relieving him of his duties as team president. In Jordan's three years with the Wizards, the first as president, the last two as a player, the team won 110 and lost 179 games. He was criticized and second-guessed about some of his personnel decisions, as well as his choice of Leonard Hamilton as coach. But during his time on the team, Jordan gave the team a national identity, which it lacked, and made it a drawing card. It is estimated that Jordan was worth between $40 and $60 million to the Wizards franchise during the two years he played. But regardless of the plusses and minuses of his time in Washington, he was now forced to move on and consider his future. Jordan's main goal was to have majority ownership in an NBA franchise, a team that he could mold given all that he learned from his days on the court.

10

A CAREER FOR THE AGES

From the moment he became famous—by making the game-winning shot for North Carolina in the 1982 NCAA Championship game against Georgetown—until he retired, for the third time, in 2003, Michael Jordan has never ceased to amaze, excel, and push himself and his game to new heights.

Despite his many talents and accomplishments, he never stopped trying to improve himself. He worked every bit as hard in practice as he did during a game. His determination and drive rubbed off on his teammates. For someone who is recognized for his numerous individual honors, Jordan is also regarded as the ultimate team player; someone who made his teammates better; someone who was a winner; and someone who managed to keep it all in perspective.

"I can't say there isn't an ego boost or a higher sense of confidence in yourself when you have had as many lights shining on you as I have had," Jordan wrote. "But I never believed all the press clippings and I never found comfort in the spotlight. I don't know how you can and not lose your work ethic. I listened, I was aware of my success, but I never stopped trying to get better."

The list of his achievements proves the point: NBA MVP five times (1988, 1991, 1992, 1996, 1998), NBA Finals MVP six times (1991–93, 1996–98), All-NBA first team 10 times (1987–93, 1996–98), NBA All-Defensive first team nine times (1988–93, 1996–98), NBA Defensive Player of the Year (1988), NBA scoring champ 10 times (1987–93, 1996–98) and NBA All-Star team 13 times (1985, 1987–93, 1996–98, 2002–03).

In 1996, in conjunction with the 50th anniversary of the NBA, Jordan was named one of the 50 Greatest Players in NBA History. In 1999, ESPN named him Athlete of the Century. His 32,292 career points rank third of all time, behind Kareem Abdul-Jabbar and Karl Malone. He holds the record for career scoring average (31.5 points a game) and the most seasons leading the league in scoring (10). He shares the record for most consecutive seasons leading the league in scoring (7) with Wilt Chamberlain.

But what means as much to Jordan as anything are the championship teams he has been a part of: North Carolina, 1982 NCAA champs; U.S. Olympic team, 1984 and

1992 gold medal winners; Chicago Bulls, six-time NBA champs.

Because he was an all-around player, who was a force on both ends of the floor, many consider him to be the greatest ever to play the game. In his book, *For the Love of the Game,* Jordan gives his own opinion on the subject:

> There is no such thing as a perfect basketball player, and I don't believe there is only one greatest basketball player. Everyone plays in different eras. I built my talents on the shoulders of someone else's talent. I believe greatness is an evolutionary process that changes and evolves era to era. Without Julius Erving, David Thompson, Walter Davis and Elgin Baylor, there never would have been a Michael Jordan. I evolved from them. They presented a challenge, the example I could improve upon. I had the idea that "I have to be better than David Thompson. I have to be better than Julius Erving. I have to be better than Magic Johnson." Those were the guiding forces in my development and I used them as motivation.
>
> We have seen different aspects of greatness in different bodies. Now we have seen many of those same aspects in one body. I'm certain down the road even more greatness will be seen in a single player. It used to be that great offensive players never played great

Michael Jordan never ceased to amaze, excel, and push himself and his game to new heights. (Associated Press)

defense. There was a driving force in me to prove that notion wrong. . . . But somebody will come along who plays even better offense and defense than me.

The evolution of greatness doesn't stop with me just as it didn't stop with Baylor, Dr. J, Larry Bird or Magic. The nature of evolution is to continue. We have all passed something along through our performance and all that has been written. . . . Evolution knows no bounds. Unless they change the height of the basket or otherwise alter the dimensions of the game, there will be a player much greater than me.

If that is the case, fans around the world should hope to be around to watch.

TIME LINE

1963   Born on February 17 in Brooklyn, New York, to James and Deloris Jordan

1982   As a freshman at North Carolina University, hits game-winning jump shot to give North Carolina a victory over Georgetown in the NCAA Championship

1984   Plays on U.S. men's Olympic basketball team; selected third overall in the NBA draft by the Chicago Bulls; signs endorsement contract with Nike, which develops the "Air Jordan" sneaker

1985   Named NBA Rookie of the Year

1988   Wins first of five MVP Awards and only Defensive Player of the Year award

1989   Marries Juanita Vanoy

1991   Scores 30 points as the Bulls beat the Lakers in Game 5 of the NBA Finals

1992   Leads Bulls over the Portland Trail Blazers to second NBA title; Helps United States win gold medal at the 1992 Olympics

1993   Chicago Bulls win third straight NBA championship, over the Phoenix Suns; Jordan's father is found murdered; stuns the sports world by announcing his retirement.

1994   Signs a free agent contract with the Chicago White Sox of the American League and is invited to spring training; Jordan starts his first professional baseball game, playing right field for the Birmingham Barons of Class AA Southern League

1995   Leaves White Sox spring training camp, because of a players' strike; returns to the Bulls and scores 19 points

1996   Leads the Bulls over the Seattle Supersonics in the NBA Finals in his first full season back since retirement; scores 25,000th career point in San Antonio; stars in film *Space Jam*

1997   Bulls win their second straight NBA title, defeating the Utah Jazz in six games; named one of the NBA's 50 greatest players

1998   Scores 41 points against the Minnesota Timberwolves to become the third player in NBA history to
reach 29,000 career points; Bulls wins third straight
NBA title and sixth in eight years, beating the Jazz

1999   Announces retirement at a news conference in
Chicago; named Athlete of the Century by ESPN,
beating out Babe Ruth

2000   Joins Washington Wizards as president of basketball operations and part owner

2001   Signs two-year contract to play for Wizards

2003   Plays final game of his career, against the Philadelphia 76ers; not rehired by Wizards as president of
basketball operations

HOW TO BECOME A PROFESSIONAL ATHLETE

THE JOB

Unlike amateur athletes who play or compete in amateur circles for titles or trophies only, professional athletic teams compete against one another to win titles, championships, and series; team members are paid salaries and bonuses for their work.

The athletic performances of individual teams are evaluated according to the nature and rules of each specific sport: Usually the winning team compiles the highest score, as in football, basketball, and soccer. Competitions are organized by local, regional, national, and international organizations and associations, whose primary functions are to promote the sport and sponsor competitive events. Within a professional sport there are usually different levels of competition based on age, ability, and gender. There are often different designations and divisions within one sport. Professional baseball, for example, is made up of the two major leagues (American and National) each made up of three divisions, East, Central, and West, and the minor leagues (Single-A, Double-A, Triple-A). All of these teams are considered professional because the players are compensated for their work, but the financial rewards are the greatest in the major leagues.

Whatever the team sport, most team members specialize in a specific area of the game. In gymnastics, for example, the entire six-member team trains on all of the gymnastic apparatuses—balance beam, uneven bars, vault, and floor exercise—but usually each of the six gymnasts excels in only one or two areas. Those gymnasts who do excel in all four events are likely to do well in the individual, all-around title, which is a part of the team competition. Team members in football, basketball, baseball, soccer, and hockey all assume different positions, some of which change depending on whether or not the team is trying to score a goal (offensive positions) or prevent the opposition from scoring one (defensive positions). During team practices, athletes focus on their specific role in a game, whether that is defensive, offensive, or both. For example, a pitcher will spend some time running bases and throwing to other positions, but the majority of his or her time will most likely be spent practicing pitching.

Professional teams train for most of the year, but unlike athletes in individual sports, the athletes who are members of a team usually have more of an off-season. Professional athletes' training programs differ according to the season. Following an off-season, most team sports have a training season in which they begin to increase the intensity of their workouts after a period of relative inactivity, in order to develop or maintain strength, cardiovascular ability, flexibility, endurance, speed, and quickness, as well as to focus on technique and control. During the season the team coach, physician, trainers, and physical therapists organize specific routines, programs, or exercises to target game skills as well as individual athletic weaknesses, whether skill-related or from injury.

These workouts also vary according to the difficulty of the game schedule. During a playoff or championship series, the coach and athletic staff realize that a rigorous workout in between games might tax the athletes' strength, stamina, or even mental preparedness, jeopardizing the outcome of the next game. Instead, the coach might prescribe a mild workout followed by intensive stretching. In addition to stretching and exercising the specific muscles used in any given sport, athletes concentrate on developing excellent eating and sleeping habits that will help them remain in top condition throughout the year. Abstaining from drinking alcoholic beverages during a season is a practice to which many professional athletes adhere.

The coaching or training staff often films the games and practices so that the team can benefit from watching their individual exploits, as well as its combined play. By watching their performances, team members can learn how to improve their techniques and strategies. It is common for professional teams to also study other teams' moves and strategies in order to determine a method of coping with the other teams' plays during a game.

REQUIREMENTS
High School
Most professional athletes demonstrate tremendous skill and interest in their sport well before high school. High school offers student athletes the opportunity to gain experience in the field in a structured and competitive environment. Under the guidance of a coach, you can begin developing suitable training programs and learn about health, nutrition, and conditioning issues.

High school also offers you the opportunity to experiment with a variety of sports and a variety of positions within a sport. Most junior varsity and some varsity high school teams allow you to try out different positions and begin to discover whether you have more of an aptitude for the defensive dives of a goalie or for the forwards' front-line action. High school coaches will help you learn to expand upon your strengths and abilities and develop yourself more fully as an athlete. High school is also an excellent time to begin developing the concentration powers, leadership skills, and good sportsmanship necessary for success on the field.

People who hope to become professional athletes should take a full load of high school courses including four years of English, math, and science, as well as health and physical education. A solid high school education will help ensure success in college (often the next step in becoming a professional athlete) and may help you earn a college athletic scholarship. A high school diploma will certainly give you something to fall back on if an injury, a change in career goals, or other circumstance prevents you from earning a living as an athlete.

Postsecondary Training

College is important for future professional athletes for several reasons. It provides the opportunity to gain skill and strength in your sport before you try to succeed in the pros, and it also offers you the chance of being observed by professional scouts.

Perhaps most important, a college education provides you with a valuable degree that you can use if you do not earn a living as a professional athlete or after your professional career ends. College athletes major in everything from communications to premed and enjoy careers as coaches, broadcasters, teachers, doctors, actors, and businesspeople, to name a few. As with high school sports, college athletes must maintain certain academic standards in order to be permitted to compete in intercollegiate play.

Other Requirements

If you want to be a professional athlete, you must be fully committed to succeeding. You must work almost nonstop to improve your conditioning and skills, and not give up when you do not succeed as quickly or as easily as you had hoped. And even then, because the competition is so fierce, the goal of earning a living as a professional athlete is still difficult to reach. For this reason, professional athletes must not get discouraged easily. They must have the self-confidence and ambition to keep working and keep trying. Professional athletes also must have a love for their sport that compels them to want to reach their fullest potential.

EXPLORING

Students interested in pursuing a career in professional sports should start playing that sport as much and as early as possible. Most junior high and high schools have well-established programs in the sports that are played at the professional level.

If a team sport does not exist in your school that does not mean your chances of playing it have evaporated. Petition your school board to establish it as a school sport and set aside funds for it. In the meantime organize other students into a club team, scheduling practices and unofficial games. If the sport is a recognized team sport in the United States or Canada, contact the sport's professional organization for additional information; if anyone would have helpful tips for gaining recognition, the professional organization would. Also, try calling the local or state athletic board to see whether or not any other schools in your area recognize it as a team sport, and make a list of those teams and try scheduling exhibition games with them. Your goal is to show your school or school board that other students have a definite interest in the game and that other schools recognize it.

To determine if you really want to commit to pursuing a professional career in your team sport, talk to coaches, trainers, and any athletes who are currently pursuing a professional career. You can also contact professional organizations and associations for information on how to best prepare for a career in their sport. Sometimes there are specialized training programs available, and the best way to find out is to get in contact with the people whose job it is to promote the sport.

EMPLOYERS

Professional athletes are employed by private and public ownership groups throughout the United States and Canada. At the highest male professional level, there are 32 National Football League franchises, 30 Major League Baseball franchises, 29 National Basketball Association franchises, 30 National Hockey League franchises, and 10 Major League Soccer franchises. The Women's National Basketball Association has 16 franchises.

STARTING OUT

Most team sports have some official manner of establishing which teams acquire which players; often this is referred to as a *draft,* although sometimes members of a professional team are chosen through a competition. Usually the draft occurs between the college and professional levels of the sport. The National Basketball Association (NBA), for example, has its NBA College Draft. During the draft the owners and managers of professional basketball teams choose players in an order based on the team's performance in the previous season. This means that the team with the worst record in the previous season has a greater chance of getting to choose first from the list of available players.

Furthermore, professional athletes must meet the requirements established by the organizing bodies of their respective sport. Sometimes this means meeting a physical requirement, such as age, height, and weight; sometimes it means fulfilling a number of required stunts, or participating in a certain number of competitions. Professional organizations usually arrange it so that athletes can build up their skills and level of play by participating in lower-level competitions. College sports, as mentioned before, are an excellent way to improve one's skills while pursuing an education.

ADVANCEMENT

Professional athletes in team sports advance in three ways: when their team advances, when they are traded to better teams, and when they negotiate better contracts. In all three instances, the individual team member who works and practices hard, and who gives his or her best performance in game after game, achieves this. Winning teams also receive a deluge of media attention that often creates celebrities out of individual players, which in turn provides these top players with opportunities for financially rewarding commercial endorsements.

Professional athletes are usually represented by *sports agents* in the behind-the-scenes deals that determine which teams they will be playing for and what they will be paid. These agents may also be involved with other key decisions involving commercial endorsements, personal income taxes, and financial investments of the athlete's revenues.

In the moves from high school athletics to collegiate athletics and from collegiate athletics to the pros, coaches and scouts are continually scouring the ranks of high school and college teams for new talent; they are most interested in the athletes who consistently deliver points or prevent the opposition from scoring. There is simply no substitute for success.

A college education, however, can prepare all athletes for the day when their bodies can no longer compete at the top level, whether because of age or an unforeseen injury. Every athlete should be prepared to move into another career, whether it is related to the world of sports or not.

Professional athletes do have other options, especially those who have graduated from a four-year college or university. Many go into some area of coaching, sports administration, management, or broadcasting. The professional athlete's unique insight and perspective can be a real asset in these careers. Other athletes simultaneously pursue other interests, some completely unrelated to their sport, such as education, business, social welfare, or the arts. Many continue to stay involved with the sport they have loved since childhood, coaching young children or volunteering with local school teams.

EARNINGS

Today professional athletes who are members of top-level teams earn hundreds of thousands of dollars in prize money at professional competitions; the top players or athletes in each sport earn as much or more in endorsements and advertising, usually for sports-related products and services, but increasingly for products or services completely unrelated to their sport. Such salaries and other incomes are not representative of the whole field of professional athletes, but are only indicative of the fantastic revenues a few rare athletes with extraordinary talent can hope to earn. In the year 2000, athletes had median annual earnings of $43,370, according to the U.S. Department of Labor. Ten percent earned less than $13,610.

Perhaps the only caveat to the financial success of an elite athlete is the individual's character or personality. An athlete with a bad temper or who is prone to unsportsmanlike behavior may still be able to participate in team play, helping to win games and garner trophies, but he or she will not necessarily be able to cash in on the commercial endorsements. Advertisers are notoriously fickle about the spokespeople they choose to endorse products; some athletes have lost million-dollar accounts because of their bad behavior on and off the court.

WORK ENVIRONMENT

Athletes compete in many different conditions, according to the setting of the sport (indoors or outdoors) and the rules of the organizing or governing bodies. Athletes who participate in football or soccer, for example, often compete in hot, rainy, or freezing conditions, but at any point, organizing officials can call off the match, or postpone competition until the weather improves.

Indoor events are less subject to cancellation. However, since it is in the best interests of an organization not to risk the athletes' health, any condition that might adversely affect the outcome of a competition is usually reason to cancel or postpone it. The coach or team physician, on the other hand, may withdraw an athlete from a game if that athlete is injured or ill. Nerves and fear are not good reasons to default on a competition, and part of ascending into the ranks of professional athletes means learning to cope with the anxiety that comes with competition. Some athletes, however, actually thrive on the nervous tension.

In order to reach the elite level of any sport, athletes must begin their careers early. Most professional athletes have been honing their skills since they were quite young. Athletes fit hours of practice time into an already full day; many famous players practiced on their own before school, as well as for several hours after school during team practice. Competitions are often far from the young athlete's home, which means they must travel on a bus or in a van with the team and coaching staff. Sometimes young athletes are placed in special training programs far from their homes and parents. They live with other athletes training for the same sport or on the same team, and only see their parents for holidays and vacations. The separation from a child's parents and family can be difficult; often an athlete's family decides to move in order to be closer to the child's training facility.

The expenses of a sport can be overwhelming, as is the time an athlete must devote to practice and travel to and from competitions. Although most high school athletic programs pay for many expenses, if the athlete wants additional training or private coaching, the child's parents must come up with the extra money. Sometimes young athletes can get official sponsors or they might qualify for an athletic scholarship from the training program. In addition to specialized equipment and clothing, the athlete must sometimes pay for a coach, travel expenses, competition fees, and, depending on the sport, time at the facility or gym where he or she practices. Gymnasts, for example, train for years as individuals, and then compete for positions on national or international teams. Up until the time they are accepted (and usually during their participation in the team), these gymnasts must pay for their expenses—from coach to travel to uniforms to room and board away from home.

Even with the years of hard work, practice, and financial sacrifice that most athletes and their families must endure, there is no guarantee that an athlete will achieve the rarest of the rare in the sports world—financial reward. An athlete needs to truly love the sport at which he or she excels, and also have a nearly insatiable ambition and work ethic.

OUTLOOK

The outlook for professional athletes will vary depending on the sport, its popularity, and the number of positions open with professional teams. On the whole, the outlook for the field of professional sports is healthy, but the number of jobs will not increase dramatically. Some sports, however, may experience a rise in popularity, which may translate into greater opportunities for higher salaries, prize monies, and commercial endorsements.

TO LEARN MORE ABOUT PROFESSIONAL ATHLETES

BOOKS

Coffey, Wayne. *Carl Lewis: The Triumph of Discipline*. Woodbridge, Conn.: Blackbirch Press, 1993.

Freedman, Russell. *Babe Didrikson Zaharias*. New York: Clarion, 1999.

Krull, Kathleen. *Lives of the Athletes: Thrills, Spills (And What the Neighbors Thought)*. New York: Harcourt Brace, 1997.

Rudeen, Kenneth. *Jackie Robinson*. New York: HarperTrophy, 1996.

Stewart, Mark. *Tiger Woods: Driving Force*. Danbury, Conn.: Children's Press, 1999.

Updyke, Rosemary Kissinger. *Jim Thorpe, the Legend Remembered*. New York: Pelican, 1997.

WEBSITES AND ORGANIZATIONS

Young people who are interested in becoming professional athletes should contact the professional organizations for the sport in which they would like to compete, such as the National Hockey League, U.S. Tennis Association, the Professional Golfer's Association, or the National Bowling Association. Ask for information on requirements, training centers, coaches, and so on.

For a free brochure and information on the Junior Olympics and more, write to

Amateur Athletic Union
P.O. Box 22409
Lake Buena Vista, FL 32830
http://www.aausports.org

For additional information on athletics

American Alliance for Health, Physical Education, Recreation, and Dance
1900 Association Drive
Reston, VA 20191
http://www.aahperd.org

The popular magazine *Sports Illustrated for Kids* also has a website.

Sports Illustrated for Kids

http://www.sikids.com

Visit the U.S. Olympic Committee's website for the latest sporting news and information about upcoming Olympic competitions.

United States Olympic Committee

http://www.olympic-usa.org

The following website provides information about and links to women in all kinds of sports:

Women in Sports

http://www.makeithappen.com/wis/index.html

HOW TO BECOME A SPORTS EXECUTIVE

THE JOB

The two top positions in most sports organizations are team president and general manager. Depending on the size of the franchise, these two positions might be blended together and held by one person.

Team presidents are the chief executive officers of the club. They are responsible for the overall financial success of the team. Presidents oversee several departments within the organization, including marketing, public relations, broadcasting, sales, advertising, ticket sales, community relations, and accounting. Since team presidents must develop strategies to encourage fans to attend games, it is good if they have some experience in public relations or marketing. Along with the public relations manager, team presidents create give-away programs, such as cap days or poster nights.

Another one of the team president's responsibilities is encouraging community relations by courting season ticket holders, as well as those who purchase luxury box seats, known as skyboxes. Usually, this involves selling these seats to corporations.

General managers handle the daily business activities of the teams, such as hiring and firing, promotions, supervising scouting, making trades, and negotiating player contracts. All sports teams have general managers, and usually the main functions of the job are the same regardless of the professional level of the team. However, some general managers that work with minor league teams might also deal with additional job duties, including managing the souvenir booths or organizing the ticket offices. The most important asset the general manager brings to an organization is knowledge of business practices. The sport can be learned later.

REQUIREMENTS
High School
High school courses that will help you to become a sports executive include business, mathematics, and

computer science. English, speech, and physical education courses will also be beneficial. Managing a school club or other organization will give you a general idea of the responsibilities and demands that this career involves.

Postsecondary Training

To become a sports executive, you will need at least a bachelor's degree. Remember, even though this is a sport-related position, presidents and general managers are expected to have the same backgrounds as corporate executives. Most have master's degrees in sports administration, and some have master's degree in business administration.

Other Requirements

Sports executives must create a positive image for their teams. In this age of extensive media coverage (including frequent public speaking engagements which are required of sports executives), excellent communications skills are a must. Sports executives need to be dynamic public speakers. They also need a keen business sense and an intimate knowledge of how to forge a good relationship with their communities. They also should have excellent organizational skills, be detail oriented, and be sound decision-makers.

EXPLORING

One way to start exploring this field is to volunteer to do something for your school's sports teams, for example, chart statistics or take on the duties of equipment manager. This is a way to begin learning how athletic departments work. Talk to the general manager of your local minor league baseball club, and try to get a part-time job with the team during the summer. When you are in college, try to get an internship within the athletic department to supplement your course of study. Any way you can gain experience in any area of sports administration will be valuable to you in your career as a sports executive. You may also find it helpful to read publications such as *Sports Business Journal* (http://www.sportsbusinessjournal.com).

EMPLOYERS

Employers include professional, collegiate, and minor league football, hockey, baseball, basketball, soccer, and other sports teams. They are located across the United States and the world. About 11 percent of all athletes, coaches, and sports officials and related workers are employed in the commercial sports industry.

STARTING OUT

A majority of all sports executives begin their careers as interns. Interning offers the opportunity to gain recognition in an otherwise extremely competitive industry. Internships vary in length and generally include college credits. They are available in hundreds of sports categories and are offered by more than 90 percent of existing sports organizations. If you are serious about working in the sports industry, an internship is the most effective method of achieving your goals.

Entry-level positions in the sports industry are generally reserved for individuals with intern or volunteer experience. Once you have obtained this experience, you are eligible for thousands of entry-level positions in hundreds of fields. Qualified employees are hard to find in any industry, so the experience you have gained through internships will prove invaluable at this stage of your career.

ADVANCEMENT

The experience prerequisite to qualify for a management-level position is generally three to five years in a specific field within the sports industry. At this level, an applicant should have experience managing a small to medium-sized staff and possess specific skills, including marketing, public relations, broadcasting, sales, advertising, publications, sports medicine, licensing, and specific sport player development.

The minimum experience to qualify for an executive position is generally seven years. Executives with proven track records in the minors can be promoted to positions in the majors. Major league executives might receive promotions in the form of job offers from more prestigious teams.

EARNINGS

General managers, team presidents, and other sports executives earn salaries that range from $20,000 to $50,000 per year in the minor leagues to more than $1 million in the majors. Most sports executives are eligible for typical fringe benefits including medical and dental insurance, paid sick and vacation time, and access to retirement savings plans.

WORK ENVIRONMENT

Sports team management is a fickle industry. When a team is winning, everyone loves the general manager or team president. When the team is losing, fans and the media often take out their frustrations on the team's executives. Sports executives must be able to handle that pressure. This industry is extremely competitive, and executives might find themselves without a job several times in their careers. Sports executives sleep, eat, and breathe their jobs, and definitely love the sports they manage.

OUTLOOK

The U.S. Department of Labor predicts that employment in amusement and recreation services (a category that includes sports-related careers) will grow by about 35 percent through 2010.

Although there are more sports executive positions available due to league expansion and the creation of new leagues, such as the Women's National Basketball Association, there still remain only a finite number of positions, and the competition for these jobs is very fierce.

TO LEARN MORE ABOUT SPORTS EXECUTIVES

BOOKS

Carter, David M., and Darrenn Rovell. *On the Ball: What You Can Learn about Business from America's Sports Leaders.* Englewood Cliffs, N.J.: Financial Times/Prentice Hall, 2003.

Ramsay, Jack. *Dr. Jack's Leadership Lessons Learned from a Lifetime in Basketball.* Hoboken, N.J.: John Wiley & Sons, 2003.

Steiner, Brandon. *The Business Playbook: Leadership Lessons from the World of Sports.* Entrepreneur Press, 2003.

WEBSITES AND ORGANIZATIONS

For information on educational programs, contact

Sports Administration Specialization Coordinator

The University of North Carolina

Department of Exercise and Sport Science

209 Fetzer Gymnasium, CB#8700

Chapel Hill, NC 27599

Tel: 919-962-0017

http://www.unc.edu/depts/exercise

To learn more about sports executives, contact

Teamwork Online LLC

22550 McCauley Road

Shaker Heights, OH 44122

Tel: 216-360-1790

Email: info@teamworkonline.com

http://www.teamworkonline.com

TO LEARN MORE ABOUT MICHAEL JORDAN

BOOKS

Bowers, Matt, ed. *2003-04 Carolina Basketball Media Guide*. Chapel Hill, N.C.: UNC Athletic Communications Office.

Chansky, Art. *The Dean's List: A Celebration of Tar Heel Basketball and Dean Smith*. New York: Warner Books, 1997.

Christopher, Matt. *On the Court with ... Michael Jordan*. Boston: Little Brown, 1996.

Hubbard, Jan, ed. *The Official NBA Basketball Encyclopedia*. New York: Doubleday, 2000.

Jordan, Michael. *For the Love of the Game: My Story*. New York: Crown Publishers, 1998.

Krugel, Mitchell. *One Last Shot: The Story of Michael Jordan's Comeback*. Thomas Dunne Books, 2002.

MacCambridge, Michael, ed. *ESPN SportsCentury*. New York: Hyperion, 1999.

McGovern, Mike. *Amazing Athletes of the 20th Century*. New York: Checkmark Books, 2002.

Smith, Ron, ed. *Sporting News Books: Official NBA Register, 2003-2004 Edition*. New York: McGraw Hill, 2003.

WEBSITES AND ORGANIZATIONS

ESPN

http://www.espn.com

Information about all sports.

Michael Jordan Official Website

http://jordan.sportsline.com

Information about Michael Jordan and his career

NBA.com

http://www.nba.com

The official site of the National Basketball Association.

Sports Illustrated

http://www.si.com

Archived articles about Michael Jordan's career.

Naismith Memorial Basketball Hall of Fame

1000 West Columbus Avenue

Springfield, MA 01105

413-781-6500

http://www.hoophall.com

A museum of basketball history, honoring its greatest players and coaches.

United Center

1901 West Madison Street

Chicago, IL 60612

312-455-4500

http://www.unitedcenter.com

The home of the Chicago Bulls.

INDEX

Page numbers in *italics* indicate illustrations.

ABOUT THE AUTHOR

Mike McGovern is an assistant sports editor and columnist at the *Reading Eagle,* a midsize daily newspaper in Reading, Pennsylvania. He has twice been named one of the top 10 sports columnists in the United States (circulation, 40,000-100,000) by the Associated Press Sports Editors. He is a three-time winner of the Keystone Award, presented by the Pennsylvania Newspaper Association, and his work has been honored by the Society of Professional Journalists (Philadelphia chapter), the Associated Press Managing Editors and the Golf Writers Association of America. He has written *The Encyclopedia of 20th Century Athletes* and *Amazing Athletes of the 20th Century* (paperback edition), and *The Complete Idiot's Guide to Sports History and Trivia.* He also co-authored *The Quotable Athlete,* with his wife, Susan Shelly. He lives in Shillington, Pennsylvania, with his wife and two children.